U0936513

最高人民法院
工作报告

2020

REPORT ON THE WORK
OF
THE SUPREME PEOPLE'S COURT

人民法院出版社

图书在版编目（CIP）数据

最高人民法院工作报告．2020：汉英对照．-- 北京：人民法院出版社，2020.7

ISBN 978-7-5109-2898-7

Ⅰ．①最… Ⅱ．Ⅲ．①最高法院－工作报告－中国－2020－汉、英 Ⅳ．① D926.21

中国版本图书馆 CIP 数据核字 (2020) 第 118741 号

最高人民法院工作报告 · 2020

责任编辑 陈晓璇 **装帧设计** 孙 宇 丁 鼎 尹苗苗 王子莹

出版发行 人民法院出版社

地　　址 北京市东城区东交民巷 27 号（100745）

电　　话（010）67550520（责任编辑） 67550558（发行部查询）
65223677（读者服务部）

客服 QQ 2092078039

网　　址 http://www.courtbook.com.cn

E－mail courtpress@sohu.com

印　　刷 北京雅昌艺术印刷有限公司

经　　销 新华书店

开　　本 787 毫米 ×1092 毫米 1/16

字　　数 76 千字

印　　张 7

版　　次 2020 年 7 月第 1 版 2020 年 7 月第 1 次印刷

书　　号 ISBN 978-7-5109-2898-7

定　　价 38.00 元

目　录

CONTENTS

扫码看报告

最高人民法院工作报告

——2020 年 5 月 25 日在第十三届全国人民代表大会第三次会议上

最高人民法院院长　周　强

各位代表：

我代表最高人民法院向大会报告工作，请予审议，并请全国政协各位委员提出意见。

新冠肺炎疫情发生以来，习近平总书记亲自指挥、亲自部署，以习近平同志为核心的党中央团结带领全党全军全国各族人民众志成城、顽强拼搏，经过艰苦卓绝的努力，武汉保卫战、湖北保卫战取得决定性成果，疫情防控阻击战取得重大战略成果，统筹推进疫情防控和经济社会发展工作取得积极成效。这些重大成果的取得，根本在于以习近平同志为核心的党中央坚强领导，充分显示了中国共产党领导和我国社会主义制度的巨大优越性，向世界展现了中国力量、中国精神、中国效率。

最高人民法院坚决贯彻习近平总书记重要指示精神和党中央决策部署，在中央政法委领导下，认真落实依法防控要求，单独或会同有关单位制定依法惩治妨害疫情防控犯罪、惩治妨害国境卫生检疫犯罪、保障复工复产等意见，完善服务“六稳”“六保”司法举措，发布57个惩处涉疫犯罪和服务复工复产典型案例，努力为抗疫护航、为大局服务。各级法院统筹做好疫情防控和维护稳定等工作，审结各类涉疫案件2736件，促进涉疫矛盾纠纷源头预防化解；严惩侵害医务工作者人身安全和人格尊严犯罪，保护抗疫中负重前行的“最美逆行者”；坚持审慎善意文明司法，积极为中小微企业纾困解难；运用远程立案、网上审判、智慧执行及时定分止争。智慧法院在疫情防控期间“大显身手”，全国法院网上立案136万件、开庭25万次、调解59万次，电子送达446万次，网络查控266万件，司法网拍成交额639亿元，执行到位金额2045亿元。广大法院干警特别是湖北和武汉法院干警坚决响应党中央号令，积极投身各地抗疫一线，为统筹推进疫情防控和经济社会发展工作提供了司法服务和保障，体现了忠于党、忠于国家、忠于人民、忠于法律的政治本色。

2019年主要工作

2019年，最高人民法院坚持以习近平新时代中国特色社会主义思想为指导，在以习近平同志为核心的党中央坚强领导下，在全国人大及其常委会有力监督下，增强“四个意识”、坚定“四个自信”、做到“两个维护”，全面贯彻党的十九大和十九届二中、三中、四中全会精神，深入贯彻习近平总书记主持中央政治局常委会会议听取最高人民法院党组工作汇报时的重要讲话精神，认真落实十三届全国人大二次会议决议，紧紧围绕“努力让人民群众在每一个司法案件中感受到公平正义”目标，坚持服务大局、司法为民、公正司法，忠实履行宪法法律赋予的职责，推动各项工作取得新成效，为经济社会发展提供有力司法服务和保障。最高人民法院受理案件38498件，审结34481件，同比分别上升10.7%和8.2%，制定司法解释20件，发布指导性案例33个，加强对全国法院审判工作的监督指导；地方各级法院受理案件3156.7万件，审结、执结2902.2万件，结案标的额6.6万亿元，同比分别上升12.7%、15.3%和20.3%。

一、全面贯彻总体国家安全观，推动建设更高水平的平安中国

坚决维护国家安全和社会稳定。审结一审刑事案件129.7万件，判处罪犯166万人。依法严惩各种渗透颠覆破坏、暴力恐怖、民族分裂、宗教极端等犯罪，坚定捍卫国家政治安全和人民根本利益。始终保持对严重危害社会治安犯罪高压态势，审结严重暴力犯罪案件4.9万件，多发性侵财犯罪案件27.2万件，涉枪涉爆、涉赌涉黄犯罪案件6.5万件，严重暴力犯罪案件连续十年呈下降态势，社会治安保持平稳有序。深入开展禁毒斗争，审结毒品犯罪案件8.6万件。会同应急管理部等强化行政执法与刑事司法衔接，依法惩治安全生产违法犯罪，保障人民群众生命财产安全。会同最高人民检察院、公安部发布惩治袭警违法犯罪意见，切实维护人民警察人身安全和执法权威。依法审理劫持公交车撞人、校园门口砍杀无辜、杀害顺风车乘客等一批重大恶性案件，对罪行极其严重的犯罪分子依法判处死刑，充分发挥刑罚震慑作用。

深入开展扫黑除恶专项斗争。坚决贯彻依法严惩方针，全国法院审结涉黑涉恶犯罪案件12639件83912人。依法审理孙小果案、杜少平操场埋尸案，对主犯孙小果、杜少平坚决判处并执行死刑，让正义最终得以实现。会同有关单位出台办理恶势力、“套路贷”、非法放贷等刑事案件意见，明确政策法律界限，确保打得狠、打得准。坚决“打伞破网”，严惩公职人员涉黑涉恶犯罪。实行“打财断血”，综合运用判处财产刑、追缴、没收违法所得等手段，彻底铲除黑恶势力经济基础。专项斗争开展以来，依法惩处了一批作恶多端的“沙霸”“路霸”“菜霸”“村霸”，净化了社会风气。

保持惩治腐败高压态势。审结贪污贿赂、渎职等案件2.5万件2.9万人，其中被告人原为中管干部的27人。准确体现宽严相济刑事政策，对艾文礼等主动投案被告人依法从宽处理，对邢云等严重腐败分子适用终身监禁。与国家监察委员会等完善国家监察与刑事司法衔接机制。积极配合境外追逃追赃，审结外逃腐败分子回国受审案件321件，依法没收彭旭峰等人转移至境外的违法所得，决不让腐败分子逍遥法外、逃避惩罚。

切实维护人民群众安全感。严惩危害食品药品安全犯罪，依法审理长生疫苗案、肖平辉生产销售注水牛肉案等重大案件，依法惩治销售地沟油等犯罪行为，维护人民群众针尖上舌尖上的安全。河北、上海、江苏等地法院依法审理涉及未经批准进口仿制药刑事案件，准确把握罪与非罪界限，让司法既有力度也不失温度。针对民族资产解冻类电信网络诈骗高发态势，会同公安部等出台意见，加大惩处力度。严惩“校园贷”犯罪，保护学生合法权益。严惩暴力伤医犯罪，对杀害北京民航总医院医生的孙文斌等一批犯罪分子依法判处并执行死刑，切实保护医务人员人身安全和合法权益，维护正常医疗秩序。针对高空抛物坠物严重威胁群众安全问题，出台司法政策，加强依法惩治和源头预防，公开审判一批高空抛物危害公共安全案件，守护人民群众头顶上的安全。

依法裁定特赦。认真落实习近平主席特赦令和全国人大常委会特赦决定，在新中国成立70周年前夕，依法裁定特赦罪犯23593人，彰显了党和国家法安天下、德润人心的仁政。

加强人权司法保障。坚持实事求是、有错必纠，各级法院按照审判监督程序再审改判刑事案件1774件，山东等法院依法纠正张志超等重大冤错案件。审结国家赔偿案件1.8万件，保障赔偿请求人合法权益。坚持罪刑法定、疑罪从无、证据裁判，依法宣告637名公诉案件被告人和751名自诉案件被告人无罪。陕西法院依法宣告范太应无罪，避免了重大冤错案件发生。坚持宽严相济刑事政策，该严则严，当宽则宽，罚当其罪。深入推进以审判为中心的刑事诉讼制度改革，全面准确适用认罪认罚从宽制度。会同司法部推进刑事案件律师辩护全覆盖，保障律师依法履职。

二、坚定不移贯彻新发展理念，服务经济社会持续健康发展

营造法治化营商环境。法治是最好的营商环境。各级法院审结一审商事案件453.7万件。制定服务高质量发展意见，出台公司法、破产法司法解释，发布民商事审判工作会议纪要，统一法律适用和裁判尺度，增强司法透明度和可预期性。依法审理涉“放管服”改革行政诉讼案件，支持监督行政机关依法行政，审结

一审行政案件28.4万件，助推法治政府建设，优化发展软环境。世界银行2020年营商环境报告显示，我国营商环境世界排名大幅跃升，“执行合同”“办理破产”“保护中小投资者”等与司法密切相关的指标明显提高，其中“司法程序质量”领先，被评价为这一领域的“全球最佳实践者”。

依法平等保护各类市场主体合法权益。坚持各类市场主体诉讼地位、法律适用、法律责任一律平等，不论国企民企、内资外资、大中小微企业，一视同仁、依法保护。坚持以发展眼光看待处理民营企业和企业家过去经营中的不规范行为，依法甄别纠正历史形成的涉产权冤错案件，苏州中院再审改判倪菊葆案，坚持全错全纠，部分错部分纠，错到哪里纠到哪里。对新中国成立以来所有司法解释进行清理，废止103件，废除一切对民营企业的不平等规定。严禁超标的查封扣押冻结财产，创新适用“活封活扣”等强制措施，尽可能减少对企业经营的影响。严格区分经济纠纷与经济犯罪、民事责任与刑事责任、合法财产与违法所得、公司财产与个人财产、正当融资与非法集资，对事实不清、证据不足案件的被告人坚决无罪释放，保护企业家人身和财产安全，激发创新创业活力。

加强知识产权司法保护。知识产权保护是创新源动力的基本保障，保护知识产权就是保护创新、促进创新。审结专利、商标、著作权等知识产权案件41.8万件，服务创新驱动发展。最高人民法院知识产权法庭依法公正高效审理发明、实用新型专利等上诉案件，促进优化科技创新法治环境。公正审理电商平台滥用市场支配地位、不正当竞争等案件，维护市场公平竞争秩序。积极适用惩罚性赔偿制度，加大侵权违法成本。福建、广东法院妥善审理高通与苹果、华为与三星系列专利纠纷案，促使当事人达成全球和解。世界知识产权组织专门出版中国知识产权司法案例。我国已成为审理知识产权案件尤其是专利案件最多的国家，也是审理周期最短的国家之一。

服务防范化解金融风险。出台司法解释，依法惩治操纵证券期货市场、内幕交易犯罪。会同人民银行、银保监会、证监会推进金融纠纷多元化解，依法保护投资者、金融消费者等各方当事人合法权益。为设立科创板并试点注册制改革制定司法保障意见，服务资本市场基础性制度改革。北京、上海等地法院有序推进“e租宝”等涉互联网金融案件清偿工作，依法参与涉金融风险重大案件处置。云南等法院依法审理“泛亚有色”等非法集资案件，积极追缴处置涉案财产，努力帮助群众挽回损失。上海金融法院创新证券纠纷示范判决机制，探索中小投资者司法保护新路径。

服务脱贫攻坚战。落实落细服务乡村振兴司法政策，依法严惩涉农骗补骗保、扶贫领域腐败、农资造假等侵害群众利益犯罪。山西、湖南、四川、宁夏等地法院妥善审理农村土地流转、林权转让、股份合作等案件，维护农村经营主体合法权益，助力贫困地区产业振兴。贵州、西藏以及怒江、临夏等地法院积极服务易地扶贫搬迁工作，维护广大农民土地承包经营权、宅基地使用权，有效化解农产品产销纠纷，促进农村经济社会发展。

服务打好蓝天碧水净土保卫战。审结一审环境资源案件26.8万件。审结检察机关和社会组织提起的环境公益诉讼案件1953件，严肃追究损毁三清山巨蟒峰等破坏生态环境人员法律责任。安徽法院审理通过暗管向长江违法排放有毒物质污染环境案，让违法者既承担刑事责任，又履行生态环境修复义务。在江苏南京、甘肃兰州新设环境资源法庭，集中管辖相应省域内环境资源案件，护航生态优先、绿色发展。长江、黄河等流域相关法院加强司法协作，推进大江大河生态保护和系统治理。

服务供给侧结构性改革。会同国家发展改革委等出台加快完善市场主体退出制度改革方案，降低退出成本，促进生产要素流动和企业转型升级。充分发挥破产制度促进市场主体优胜劣汰、化解地方金融风险、维护社会和谐稳定的重要作用，妥善审结破产重整等案件4626件，涉及债权6788亿元，推动“僵尸企业”平稳有序出清，让482家有发展前景的企业通过重整走出困境，帮助10.8万名员工保住就业岗位。天津法院依法支持国企重整混改，促进化解国企债务风险。通化法院通过破产重整程序帮助通钢集团顺利实现“债转股”，化解巨额债务危机，保障了广大小额债权人和企业职工利益。淮北法院探索房企破产和解模式，促进房地产市场健康发展。

服务区域协调发展战略实施。出台专门意见，服务雄安新区规划建设和创新发展。北京、天津、河北法院妥善化解涉重大项目纠纷，服务京津冀协同发展和冬奥会冬残奥会筹办。上海、江苏、浙江、安徽法院提高司法协作水平，服务长三角区域一体化发展。辽宁、吉林、黑龙江法院聚焦优化营商法治环境，服务新时代东北全面振兴、全方位振兴。广东法院着力营造公正高效的法治环境，为粤港澳大湾区和深圳先行示范区建设护航。

服务数字经济发展。加强数据权利司法保护，有利于大数据利用、数字经济发展，有利于公民个人隐私保护。司法要为数字经济营造竞争中性、开放包容的环境。各级法院依法妥善审理涉新交易新模式新业态案件，保障数字经济健康发展，促进数字经济与实体经济深度融合，为经济高质量发展提供新动能。审理人工智能、网络游戏著作权案等一批新类型案件，加强对数字版权、数字内容产品的保护。加大数据安全和个人隐私保护力度，严惩侵犯公民个人信息犯罪，依法审理手机应用擅自读取用户通讯录信息、网络信用平台滥用个人征信数据等案件；准确适用“通知删除”规则，对散发诽谤他人言论的网络平台，根据受害人请求责令删除相关信息。

服务更高水平对外开放。审结一审涉外民商事案件1.7万件，海事海商案件1.6万件。制定外商投资法司法解释，依法平等保护中外投资者合法权益。出台服务“一带一路”建设意见、服务上海自贸试验区临港新片区建设意见。天津、湖北、广西、重庆、四川等法院积极完善自贸试验区司法保障举措。海南法院开通自贸港司法服务平台，为中外投资者免费提供司法征信服务。南京海事法院立足区位优势，积极服务海洋经济发展。青岛海事法院妥善化解“尼莉莎”轮扣押案，避免涉事各方巨额损失，外国当事人特意将轮船更名为“尊重”，向中国法治致敬。

三、坚持司法为民、公正司法，维护社会公平正义

弘扬社会主义核心价值观。高扬爱国主义旗帜，严惩侮辱国旗国徽国歌犯罪，宣示国家象征庄严神圣不可侵犯。审结英烈保护公益诉讼案件22件，对侵害方志敏、董存瑞、黄继光、木里救火牺牲勇士等英烈权益的行为，严肃追究法律责任，旗帜鲜明捍卫英烈荣光。贯彻《新时代公民道德建设实施纲要》，坚持把社会主义核心价值观融入司法工作，用法治力量引导人民群众向上向善。会同国家发展改革委等健全失信被执行人联合惩戒机制，鼓

励诚实守信，惩戒失信违约。审理网络众筹退款等案件，规范网络公益行为，守护扶危济困、诚信友善的传统美德。

维护社会公平。审结一审民事案件939.3万件，其中涉及教育、就业、医疗、住房、消费、社会保障等民生领域案件144万件。严厉惩处侵害残疾人的犯罪，方便残疾人诉讼，切实保障残疾人合法权益。积极参加“护薪”行动，加强拖欠农民工工资案件审判执行工作，加大惩处拒不支付劳动报酬犯罪力度，帮助农民工追讨欠薪106.6亿元。发放司法救助金11.2亿元，帮助涉诉困难群众摆脱困境。会同人社部等发布促进妇女平等就业规范性文件，营造公平就业制度环境。妥善审理女工怀孕被解雇、毕业生求职遭地域歧视等案件，推进城乡居民人身损害赔偿标准统一试点，依法保障权利公平、机会公平、规则公平。

促进和谐家庭建设。深化家事审判改革，会同全国妇联等健全妇女儿童权益保护机制，更加注重对家庭成员人格、安全、情感的保护。审结婚姻家庭案件185万件，加大反家暴力度，及时签发人身安全保护令2004份。河南新乡、湖北孝感、广西玉林等地法院加强婚姻家庭纠纷调解，尽可能让感情尚未破裂的夫妻重归于好，让孩子能够享受完整家庭的温暖；让感情确已破裂的夫妻解除婚姻，避免酿成家庭悲剧。严惩虐待、遗弃、伤害老年人犯罪，审结赡养案件2.6万件，维护老年人合法权益；家事法庭巧断家务事，妥善化解赡养、抚养纠纷，让中华民族尊老爱幼美德代代相传，重视家庭的传统永续绵延。

保护未成年人健康成长。完善少年司法制度，坚持圆桌式审判。广州中院陈海仪法官用母亲般的关怀帮助失足少年走向新生。通过组织观摩少年法庭，让少年体验司法，学习法律常识。依法严惩侵害少年儿童身心健康的犯罪，对性侵儿童的赵志勇、何龙等罪行极其严重的一批犯罪分子，坚决依法判处死刑。会同民政部等出台意见，加强对事实无人抚养儿童的保护，贵州等法院专门制定保护农村留守儿童合法权益文件，让每一个孩子都沐浴在法治的阳光下。加强校园欺凌预防处置，审结相关案件 4192 件。会同教育部等完善校园安全事故处理机制，依法惩治涉及“校闹”的犯罪。积极推进司法保护与行政、家庭、学校、社区保护联动机制试点，用法治呵护少年儿童健康成长。

维护国防利益和军人军属合法权益。全面完成服务保障涉军停偿工作，全国法院 5 个先进单位、15 名先进个人受到人社部和中央军委政治工作部、后勤保障部联合表彰。研究出台 15 条举措，组织专门力量，实行绿色通道，为做好涉军停偿下篇文章积极提供司法服务。严惩破坏军事设施、冒充军人招摇撞骗等犯罪，审结相关案件 484 件。军事法院稳步推开军事行政审判试点，依法维护部队官兵合法权益。湖南、重庆、四川等法院健全军地法院协作机制，山东临沂、河南信阳等法院发扬革命老区好传统好经验，用心用情用法做好涉军维权工作，促进军政军民团结。

保护港澳台同胞和海外侨胞、归侨侨眷合法权益。审结涉港澳台案件 2.7 万件，办理司法协助互助案件 9648 件，审结涉侨案件 2475 件。基本实现内地与香港民商事司法协助全覆盖。建成内地与澳门司法协助网络平台。出台司法惠台 36 条措施，平等保护台胞台企合法权益。积极为港澳台法律学生实习创造条件，增进港澳台青年对祖国司法制度的了解认识。

引导社会成员增强公共意识、规则意识。现代社会，人们工作生活离不开公共空间，规范的公共空间行为是社会充满活力、和谐有序的基础。对发生在公共空间案件的审理，人民法院兼顾国法天理人情，明辨是非，惩恶扬善，努力实现法律效果与社会效果的统一。审理“撞伤儿童离开遇阻猝死案”，判决阻拦者不担责，鼓励见义勇为。审理“患者飞踹医生反被伤案”，改判医生为正当防卫，坚决跟“和稀泥”说不。审理“微信群主踢群第一案”，支持群组内正当管理行为，不让网络社区成为法外之地。审理“私自上树摘杨梅坠亡案”，认定村委会未违反安全保障义务，让守法者不用为他人过错买单。审理“冰面遛狗溺亡索赔案”，让自甘冒险者自负其责。审理“小偷逃逸跳河溺亡案”，依法判定追赶群众无责，宣示见义勇为者不用承担过重注意义务。通过一系列案件审理，破解长期困扰群众的“扶不扶”“劝不劝”“追不追”“救不救”“为不为”“管不管”等法律和道德风险，坚决防止“谁能闹谁有理”“谁横谁有理”“谁受伤谁有理”等“和稀泥”做法，让司法有力量、有是非、有温度；让群众有温暖、有遵循、有保障，争做法治中国好公民。

四、构建便民高效的矛盾纠纷化解机制，积极参与社会治理

化解矛盾纠纷是社会治理的重要内容。人民法院是化解矛盾纠纷、解决群众诉求的审判机关。公正高效化解矛盾、定分止争，是人民法院参与社会治理的重要职责，也是推进国家治理体系和治理能力现代化的重要内容。

畅通群众纠纷解决渠道。巩固立案登记制改革成果，推进案件当场立、自助立、网上立，坚决防止立案难反弹回潮。法院敞开大门，但不能唱独角戏，必须坚持和发展新时代“枫桥经验”，

融入党委领导的社会治理体系，依靠人民群众和社会组织有效预防化解矛盾纠纷。各地法院坚持把非诉讼纠纷解决机制挺在前面，加强人民调解、行政调解、司法调解联动，非诉讼和诉讼对接，充分发挥人民法院调解平台在线化解纠纷功能，让人民内部矛盾能够更快更有效化解。云南、青海、宁夏、新疆和兵团等法院创新民族特色调解机制，维护各族群众合法权益，促进民族团结。浙江法院总结推广普陀、安吉做法，积极参与社会治理大格局，切实把矛盾解决在萌芽状态、化解在基层。

建立一站式多元解纷和诉讼服务机制。推进案件繁简分流、轻重分离、快慢分道，在诉讼服务中心建立调解、速裁、快审一站式解纷机制，为实现公平正义提速。全国法院诉讼服务中心化解案件 849.7 万件，其中速裁快审案件平均审理周期较一审民商事案件缩短 49.2%。畅通诉讼服务渠道，决不让群众无处申诉，决不许对群众诉求置之不理。在诉讼服务中心提供一站通办、一网通办、一号通办的诉讼服务，江西、湖南等地法院在乡村社区设置自助诉讼服务设施，让群众参与诉讼更加便捷。

推广跨域立案诉讼服务。在全国范围全面推开跨域立案诉讼服务，当事人可以就近选择法院提交立案申请，减少往来奔波。京津冀、长三角、珠三角地区率先实现跨域立案域内全贯通，全国中级、基层法院和海事法院实现跨域立案服务全覆盖，“家门口起诉”新模式有效解决群众异地诉讼不便问题。

立足城乡基层化解纠纷。充分发挥全国 10759 个人民法庭作用，积极参与县域基层治理，共调解、审结案件 473.1 万件。延安、寻乌、两当等地人民法庭坚持群众说事、民事直说、法官说法，及时化解矛盾纠纷，服务乡村振兴。“马背法庭”“背篓法官”

跋山涉水，深入田间地头、百姓家中，努力做到哪里有司法需求，人民法庭司法服务就跟进到哪里。

五、巩固“基本解决执行难”成果，保持执行工作高水平运行

如期实现“基本解决执行难”目标之后，人民法院咬定青山不放松，不断巩固“基本解决执行难”成果，朝着切实解决执行难目标迈进。2019 年，全国法院共受理执行案件 1041.4 万件，执结 954.7 万件，执行到位金额 1.7 万亿元，同比分别上升 17.4%、22.4% 和 10.8%，各项执行指标稳中有进，中国特色执行制度、机制和模式更加健全。

深化综合治理、源头治理。认真贯彻中央全面依法治国委员会 2019 年“1 号文件”，推动完善跨部门系统监管和联合惩戒机制，巩固拓展综合治理执行难格局。河北、江西、河南、陕西等地全面依法治省委员会制定贯彻落实意见，湖南省人大常委会专门出台文件，支持法院切实解决执行难。认真落实代表审议意见，制定实施执行工作五年发展纲要，健全长效机制，确保攻坚之后标准不降、力度不减。制定律师参与执行意见，充分发挥专业力量作用。按照全国人大常委会部署，配合开展民事强制执行法立法工作，推动健全中国特色执行法律制度。

强化善意执行、文明执行。坚持依法严格公正执行，坚决打击逃避、抗拒执行行为，保障胜诉当事人合法权益。制定强化善意文明执行意见，优化查封、变价等措施，最大限度降低对企业生产经营的影响。对资金链暂时断裂但仍有发展潜力、存在救治可能的企业，引导通过和解分期履行、兼并重组等方式执行。建

立信用惩戒分级管理和失信修复等机制，严格失信惩戒程序条件，精准实施信用惩戒。依法及时删除失信名单 208.3 万人次，同比上升 19.3%。转变执行工作理念，由过去的惩戒为主变为惩戒与激励并重，浙江宁波、福建宁德等法院推行自动履行正向激励机制，促进自动履行率大幅提升，营造了褒扬守信的社会氛围。

加大力度解决群众反映强烈的问题。针对涉民生、金融、拖欠民营企业账款等案件，集中开展专项执行行动。集中执行期间，全国法院执结涉民生案件 21 万件，执行到位金额 98 亿元，让人民群众获得感更加充实。执结涉金融案件 47 万件，执行到位金额 2000 亿元。执结拖欠民营企业账款案件 5870 件，执行到位金额 127 亿元，切实保护民营企业、中小企业合法权益。

六、深化司法体制改革和智慧法院建设，不断提高司法质量、效率和公信力

公正与效率是人民法院永恒的价值追求。面对全球范围内案件尤其民商事案件持续较快增长趋势，中国法院要提供自己的解决方案。我们既不能走不断扩编增员的路子，更不能走限制立案、选择立案、拒绝群众诉求的路子，必须靠深化司法改革、建设智慧法院，加快推进审判体系和审判能力现代化。

深化司法体制综合配套改革。贯彻政法领域全面深化改革实施意见，发布人民法院第五个五年改革纲要，促进各项改革系统集成、协同高效。贯彻新修订的人民法院组织法和法官法，健全配套机制，推动中国特色社会主义司法制度优势转化为治理效能。落实人民陪审员法，扩大参审范围，全国陪审员参审案件 340.7 万件。根据全国人大常委会授权，在 15 个省份 20 个城市开展民

事诉讼程序繁简分流改革试点，通过制度创新激发司法效能，满足群众多元、高效、便捷的纠纷解决需求。

全面落实司法责任制。健全有序放权、科学配权、规范用权、严格限权的审判权力运行体系，制定审判权力和责任清单，明确院庭长、审判组织、法官的权限和责任，压实院庭长审判监督管理职责，做到有权必有责、用权必担责、失职必问责、滥权必追责。充分发挥司法解释、指导性案例作用，推行类案与关联案件强制检索机制，完善审判委员会工作机制，促进裁判尺度统一。深化法官员额制改革，加强法官遴选工作，健全法官员额省级统筹、动态调整和交流退出机制，做到有进有出、优胜劣汰。山西、内蒙古、重庆等地落实落细履职保障政策，激励法官秉公办案、公正司法。

探索互联网司法新模式。发挥北京、杭州、广州互联网法院引领作用，推广“网上案件网上审理”，完善在线诉讼规则，让群众享受在线诉讼便利。全面推广“中国移动微法院”，推动电子诉讼服务向移动端发展，引领世界移动电子诉讼发展潮流。审理涉及“直播带货”等案件，明确网络空间行为规范、权利边界和责任。审理“暗刷流量”等互联网违法案件，促进网络空间治理法治化。在乌镇举办世界互联网法治论坛，深化互联网司法国际合作，推动构建网络空间命运共同体。

推动大数据、区块链等技术深度应用。深化司法大数据应用，完成专题报告806份，为治理高空抛物坠物、保护妇女儿童权益等提供参考。建成全国统一司法区块链平台，创新在线存证方式，推动解决电子证据取证难、存证难、认证难问题。在执行中应用区块链智能合约技术，提高执行规范化水平。推广庭审语音识别、文书智能纠错、“法信”智能推送等应用，为法官办案、群众诉讼提供智能辅助。

深化阳光司法。截至今年4月，中国裁判文书网公布文书9195万份，中国审判流程信息公开网向当事人公开案件2900万件，公开信息15亿项，让公平正义经得起围观。中国庭审公开网直播案件696万件，观看量237亿人次，在线旁听庭审成为群众尊法学法守法用法新平台。经过多年实践，开放动态透明便民的阳光司法机制更趋成熟定型，丰富发展了社会主义法治文明。

司法改革和智慧法院作为人民法院审判体系和审判能力现代化的“车之两轮、鸟之双翼”，有力提升了审判质效。2019年，全国法院法官人均办案228件，同比增长13.4%；各类案件一审后当事人服判息诉率89.2%，二审后达到98.2%；涉诉信访总量、涉诉进京访同比分别下降13.3%和40%；互联网法院案件平均审理周期42天，比传统模式缩短57.1%。

七、坚持革命化、正规化、专业化、职业化方向，大力加强人民法院队伍建设

始终把党的政治建设摆在首位。深入学习贯彻习近平新时代中国特色社会主义思想，切实用以武装头脑、指导实践、推动工作，牢牢坚持党对司法工作的绝对领导。扎实开展“不忘初心、牢记使命”主题教育，接受深刻思想政治洗礼，引导广大干警牢记初心使命、忠诚履职担当。认真落实《中国共产党政法工作条例》，把党的领导贯彻到人民法院工作各方面和全过程。坚持抓党建带队建促审判，努力创建让党中央放心、让人民群众满意的模范机关。认真接受中央巡视，狠抓问题整改。深入开展向邹碧华

学习活动，全国法院涌现出李庆军等一批新时代司法为民、公正司法的先进典型，532个集体、661名个人受到中央有关部门表彰，北京法院宋鱼水、辽宁法院谭彦、黑龙江法院孙波、上海法院邹碧华、福建法院黄志丽被授予“最美奋斗者”称号，他们以忠诚乃至生命诠释了人民法官的初心。

不断加强司法能力建设。培训干警61.5万人次。创新法治人才培养机制，深化同高校合作，积极参与中国政法实务大讲堂专题讲座，促进司法实践与教学科研紧密结合。选派851名法官参加涉外培训交流，培养专业化涉外司法人才。加强基层基础建设，改善基层工作条件，加大对革命老区、民族地区、边疆地区、贫困地区法院建设和人才培养支持力度。培养双语法官1345人，内蒙古、西藏、青海、新疆等法院积极参与“双语法律文化出版工程”，更好满足民族地区群众司法需求。

持之以恒正风肃纪。严格贯彻中央八项规定及其实施细则精神，切实解决困扰基层的形式主义、官僚主义问题。结合主题教育开展深化突出问题集中整治，切实解决“灯下黑”问题。严格落实“一岗双责”，让失责必问成为常态。坚持刀刃向内，以零容忍态度严惩司法腐败，坚决清除害群之马。最高人民法院查处本院违纪违法干警11人，各级法院查处利用审判执行权违纪违法干警1374人，其中追究刑事责任115人。针对违规过问案件、违反任职回避、充当诉讼掮客、亲友隐名代理等影响司法廉洁的突出问题，深入自查自纠，全面彻底整改。深入开展警示教育，以违纪违法案件为反面教材，深刻汲取教训，举一反三，堵塞漏洞，健全机制，营造风清气正的司法环境。

八、自觉接受监督，加强和改进人民法院工作

依法接受人大监督，认真落实十三届全国人大二次会议决议和代表提出的意见建议，逐项细化分工，加强跟踪督办。认真落实全国人大常委会关于解决执行难情况专项报告的审议意见，并专门报告落实情况。向全国人大常委会专题报告刑事审判工作情况，根据审议意见，推进新时代刑事审判工作发展。认真办理代表建议 355 件，办理日常建议 395 件，全程密切沟通，充分采纳代表意见。邀请全国人大代表视察法院、参加会议、旁听庭审等活动 1492 人次，专门邀请代表共同开展长江、黄河流域生态环境司法保护调研。认真接受民主监督，办理政协提案 173 件，走访接待全国政协委员 180 人次；加强与民主党派、工商联和无党派人士沟通，广泛听取意见。深入贯彻监察法，自觉接受监察机关对法院工作人员进行监督。依法接受检察机关诉讼监督，公正审理抗诉案件，认真办理检察建议。广泛接受社会监督，积极开展特约监督员、特邀咨询员、专家学者调研座谈、列席审委会等活动。加强与新闻媒体互动，深入开展全媒体直播活动，主动接受舆论监督。

各位代表，人民法院工作的发展进步，根本在于以习近平同志为核心的党中央坚强领导，根本在于习近平新时代中国特色社会主义思想科学指引。人民法院工作成绩的取得，是全国人大及其常委会有力监督，国务院大力支持，全国政协民主监督，国家监察委员会、最高人民检察院监督，各民主党派、工商联、人民团体、无党派人士民主监督，地方各级党政机关、全国人大代表、全国政协委员、社会各界和广大人民群众关心支持帮助的结果。在此，我代表最高人民法院表示衷心的感谢！

我们清醒认识到，人民法院工作还存在不少问题：**一是**司法理念、司法能力与新时代新要求相比还存在较大差距，应对风险挑战、服务高质量发展等方面能力还需加强。**二是**对经济社会发展给司法带来的新情况新问题研究不够，出现一些案件裁判尺度不统一问题。**三是**司法体制综合配套改革存在落实不到位情况，审判管理制度和审判权力运行监督制约机制不够健全。**四是**知识产权、互联网、涉外等领域高素质专业化审判人才短缺，人才培养机制有待改进。**五是**司法作风不正、司法腐败问题时有发生，有的干警以案谋私、权钱交易甚至充当黑恶势力“保护伞”，党风廉政建设和反腐败斗争任务依然艰巨繁重。**六是**一些法院人案矛盾突出、办案压力大，一些边远地区基层法院招人难、留人难问题突出。对这些问题，我们将在党的领导下采取有力措施，切实加以解决。

下一阶段工作安排

今年是全面建成小康社会和“十三五”规划收官之年，也是脱贫攻坚决战决胜之年。新冠肺炎疫情对我国经济社会发展带来前所未有的冲击，对国际国内形势带来前所未有的重大影响，我国发展面临的挑战前所未有，司法工作面临的挑战也前所未有，任务十分艰巨繁重。人民法院要坚持以习近平新时代中国特色社会主义思想为指导，增强“四个意识”、坚定“四个自信”、做到“两个维护”，全面贯彻党的十九大和十九届二中、三中、四中全会及中央政法工作会议精神，深入学习贯彻习近平总书记主持中央政治局常委会会议听取最高人民法院党组工作汇报时的重要讲话精神，认真落实本次大会决议，胸怀中华民族伟大复兴的战略全局和世界百年未有之大变局，坚持党对司法工作的绝对领导，坚持以人民为中心，坚持稳中求进工作总基调，善于化危为机，充分履行职责，依法维护经济发展和社会稳定大局，为统筹推进疫情防控和经济社会发展工作，确保完成决战决胜脱贫攻坚目标任务，全面建成小康社会提供有力司法服务和保障。

一是着力服务保障常态化疫情防控和全面恢复经济社会秩序。在常态化疫情防控中做好司法应对，依法保障人民生命安全和身体健康，充分发挥司法促发展、稳预期、保民生的作用，依法保障国家惠企政策有效落实，精准服务做好“六稳”工作、落实“六保”任务。坚持把非诉讼纠纷解决机制挺在前面，注重运用调解、执行和解等方式妥善化解因疫情引发的矛盾纠纷，在法治轨道上保障常态化疫情防控。依法准确适用不可抗力规则，合理平衡当事人利益，引导各方共担风险、共克时艰。坚持善意文明执行理念，坚决杜绝超标的查封、乱查封，有效运用“活封”措施，尽最大可能保持企业财产运营价值。通过破产重整、和解等程序帮助企业化解危机、脱困重生。充分运用司法手段，尽最大努力保企业特别是中小微企业生存，保障和促进就业。依法妥善化解投资消费、新型基建等领域纠纷，为实施扩大内需战略营造良好法治环境。依法打击恶意逃废债行为。依法公正高效审理各类涉外案件，服务扩大对外开放和共建“一带一路”高质量发展，支持海南自由贸易港建设。深化国际司法交流合作，推动全球抗疫法治合作，服务构建人类命运共同体。中国法院将严格遵守国际法和公认的国际关系基本原则，坚决捍卫我国司法主权和国家安全。

二是着力服务更高水平的平安中国建设。严厉打击敌对势力渗透、破坏、颠覆、分裂活动。依法惩治影响常态化疫情防控各类犯罪，坚决维护国家安全、生物安全、生态安全、公共卫生安全和社会稳定。立足司法职能推动健全公共卫生体系，强化和完善公共卫生法治保障。依法惩治职务犯罪，服务一体推进不敢腐、不能腐、不想腐。严惩公共安全、民生保障等领域犯罪，加强新型犯罪问题研究应对。强化人权司法保障，依法保障律师执业权利。深化扫黑除恶专项斗争，依法公正高效审理涉黑涉恶犯罪案件，让每一起案件都经得起法律和历史检验，让人民群众收获更多安全感。

三是着力服务经济高质量发展。紧扣决战决胜脱贫攻坚和全面建成小康社会目标任务完善司法政策，严惩“三农”领域各类犯罪，深化法治扶贫，强化消费扶贫、就业扶贫、产业扶贫司法保障，加强金融、环境资源等案件审判，为打好三大攻坚战提供有力司法服务。推广北京、上海等地法院做法，积极营造更加稳定公平透明、可预期的法治化营商环境。加强产权和知识产权司法保护，保护商业秘密。加强数据权利和个人信息安全保护，严惩泄露、倒卖等侵犯公民个人信息犯罪，服务数字经济健康发展。完善司法服务政策举措，为京津冀协同发展、粤港澳大湾区建设、长江经济带发展、长三角区域一体化发展、黄河流域生态保护和高质量发展、西部大开发、东北全面振兴、中部地区崛起、成渝地区双城经济圈建设等提供高水平司法服务。

四是着力加强民生司法保障。认真贯彻实施审议通过后的民法典，全面清理民事司法解释，制定新的配套司法解释，加强学习培训，提升民事司法能力和水平，依法保护民事主体合法权益，调整民事关系，维护社会和经济秩序。坚持把社会主义核心价值观要求融入司法审判，落实“谁执法谁普法”要求，弘扬正风正气。执行工作永远在路上，健全切实解决执行难长效机制，强化公正规范文明执行。积极参与市域社会治理，发挥人民法庭作用，服务法治乡村建设。依法维护国防利益，保障军人军属、退役军人合法权益。坚持以人民呼声为第一信号，不断解决群众关注的难点堵点痛点问题。加强妇女儿童、老年人、残疾人等的司法保护。坚决依法纠正就业中地域、性别等歧视，坚决依法纠正违反法律规定解除新冠肺炎患者劳动合同关系的行为，依法治理农民工欠薪问题，维护劳动者公平就业权利。

五是着力推进审判体系和审判能力现代化。认真实施人民法院贯彻落实党的十九届四中全会精神的意见，提升司法促进治理体系和治理能力现代化效能。加强改革“回头看”，巩固改革成果，认真落实深化司法责任制综合配套改革意见，加强对下指导，提升改革成效。深化民事诉讼程序繁简分流改革。优化行政诉讼庭审程序。全面提升一站式多元解纷和诉讼服务实效。研究新情况解决新问题，推进裁判尺度统一。深化司法公开。巩固拓展疫情期间智慧法院建设应用成果，完善互联网司法模式。

六是着力建设忠诚干净担当的过硬法院队伍。加强人民法院党的政治建设，巩固深化主题教育成果，强化人才培养和队伍管理，锻造一支政治过硬、业务过硬、责任过硬、纪律过硬、作风过硬的高素质队伍。强化基层基础建设，支持革命老区、民族地区、边疆地区、贫困地区法院发展。认真抓好巡视整改落实。自觉接受人大监督、民主监督和各方面监督。夯实全面从严治党主体责任，坚决破除形式主义、官僚主义，严格执行防止外部和内部人员干预过问司法“三个规定”等铁规禁令，让暗箱操作没有空间，让司法腐败无法藏身，扎实开展“以案释德、以案释纪、以案释法”警示教育，以零容忍态度严惩司法腐败，把“严”的主基调长期坚持下去，以廉洁司法确保公正司法。发扬斗争精神，增强斗争本领，以司法担当化解矛盾纠纷，以公正司法实现公平正义。

各位代表，做好今年人民法院工作，责任重大，使命光荣。我们要更加紧密地团结在以习近平同志为核心的党中央周围，以习近平新时代中国特色社会主义思想为指导，忠实履行宪法法律赋予的职责，坚定信心，迎难而上，埋头苦干，为实现“两个一百年”奋斗目标、实现中华民族伟大复兴的中国梦作出新的更大贡献！

附件一

一、依法服务保障统筹推进疫情防控和经济社会发展

1 制度保障

人民法院抗疫工作情况报告

- 疫情防控期间诉讼服务和申诉信访工作通告
- 依法惩治妨害疫情防控违法犯罪意见
- 疫情防控期间加强和规范在线诉讼工作通知
- 切实做好疫情期间审判执行工作通知
- 政法机关依法保障疫情防控期间复工复产意见
- 进一步加强国境卫生检疫工作依法惩治妨害国境卫生检疫违法犯罪意见
- 依法妥善审理涉疫情民事案件若干问题指导意见(一)(二)
- 依法妥善办理涉疫情执行案件若干问题指导意见

为抗疫护航
为大局服务

2 全国法院审理涉疫情案件情况

各级法院受理各类涉疫情案件**6328**件、审结**2736**件

通过执行、破产等程序保障医疗单位运行和防疫物资供应等案件**402**件

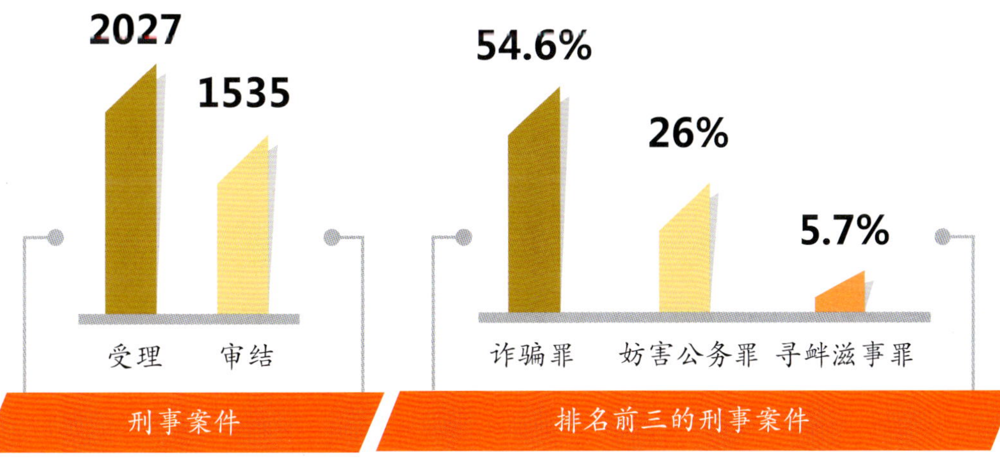

3 人民法院服务保障疫情防控和复工复产典型案例

依法惩处妨害疫情防控犯罪典型案例**3**批**26**个

服务保障疫情防控期间复工复产典型案例**3**批**31**个

依法惩处涉医犯罪典型案例**8**个

人民法院依法抗疫系列动漫

8场“抗疫前线 法治报道”全媒体直播

全景呈现司法助力统筹推进疫情防控和经济社会发展举措

4 服务保障常态化疫情防控和全面恢复经济社会秩序

精准服务“六稳”“六保”

- 依法严惩妨害疫情防控、复工复产和国境卫生检疫违法犯罪
- 准确适用不可抗力、诉讼时效等规则
- 加大产权和知识产权司法保护力度
- 坚持善意执行、文明执行
  - 乱查封
  - 超标的查封
- 依法纠正就业歧视行为
- 利用破产重整等程序帮助企业脱困重生
- 推进涉疫矛盾纠纷多元化解

5 充分运用智慧法院建设成果保障人民群众诉讼

注：以上数据统计期间为2020年2月3日至4月30日。

6 依法保护“最美逆行者”

关于做好疫情防控期间保障医务人员安全维护良好医疗秩序通知

依法严厉打击

- 暴力伤害医务人员
- 侮辱恐吓诽谤医务人员
- 故意撕扯医用防护装备
- 非法限制医务人员人身自由

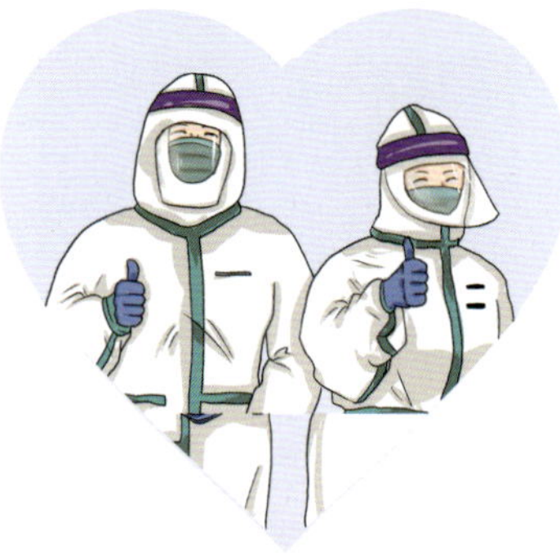

白衣执甲 逆行出征

7 各地法院抗疫举措

严惩防疫物资诈骗犯罪

严惩抗拒疫情防控措施犯罪

严惩破坏野生动物资源犯罪

纾解企业困难 保障复工复产

为坚决打赢疫情防控人民战争、总体战、阻击战提供有力司法服务和保障

二、人民法院审判执行工作

扫码看图示

1 2015–2019年最高人民法院受理、审结案件数量

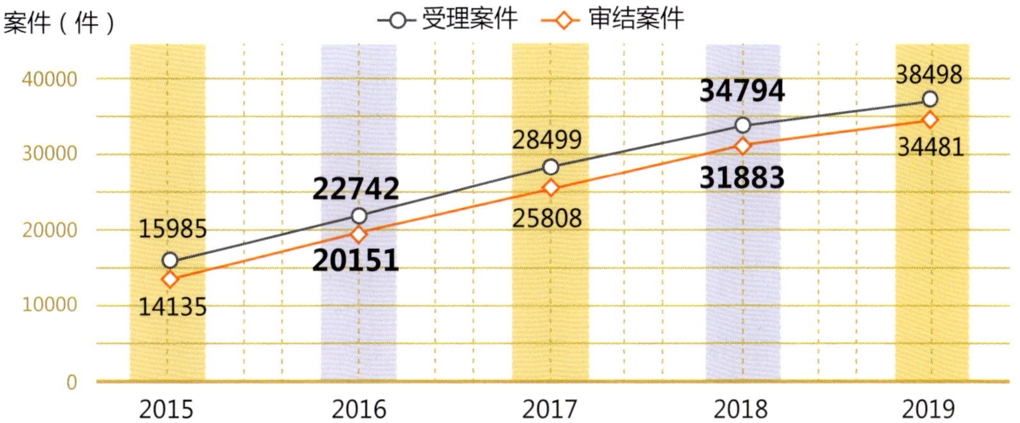

2 十年来地方各级人民法院受理、审执结案件数量

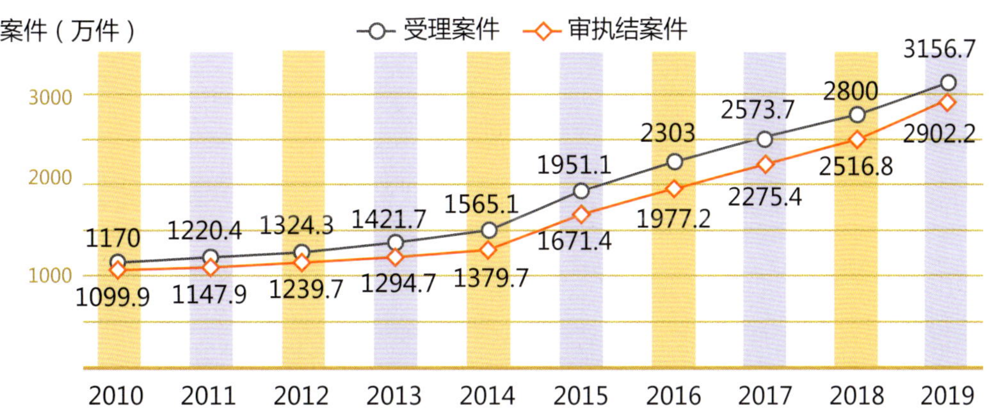

3 2019年至今人民法院工作热词

中国法院印象 · 2019

4 2016年法官员额制改革以来法官人均办案量

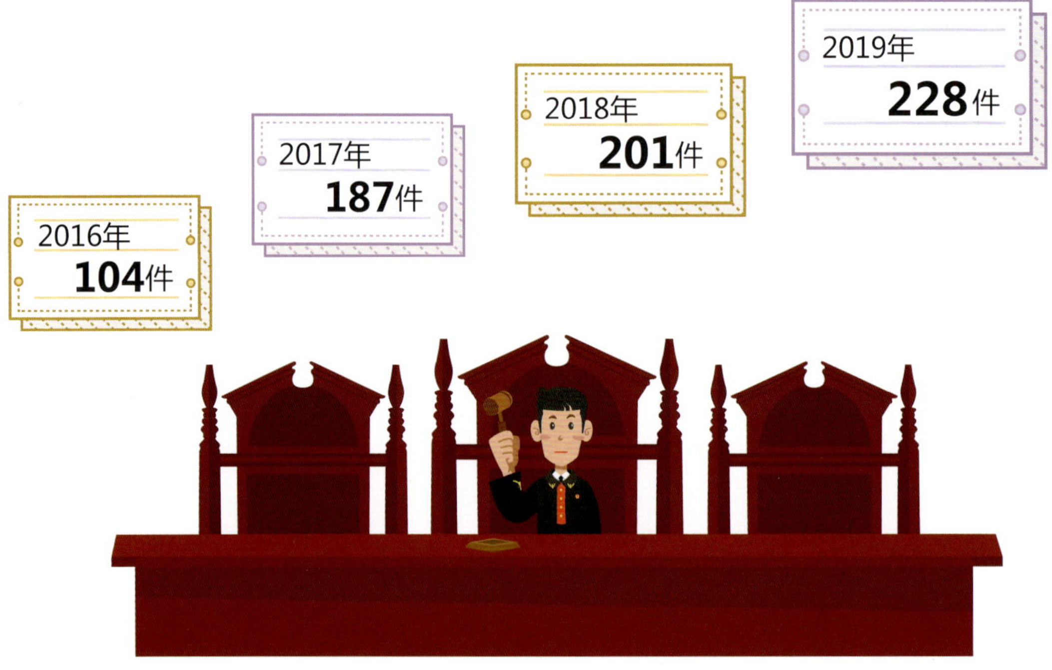

5 2019年人民法院审执结案件构成

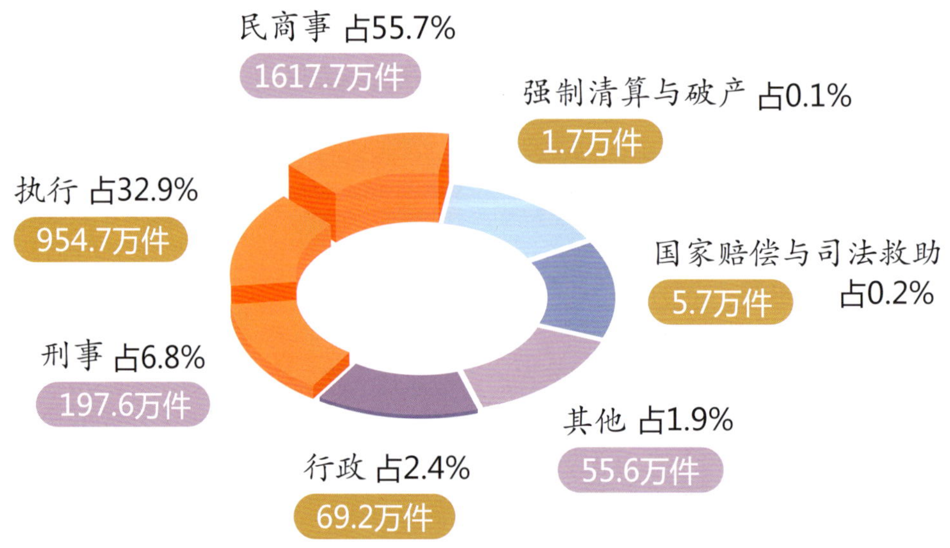

注："其他"包括管辖、司法协助等案件。

6 2019年一审刑事案件构成

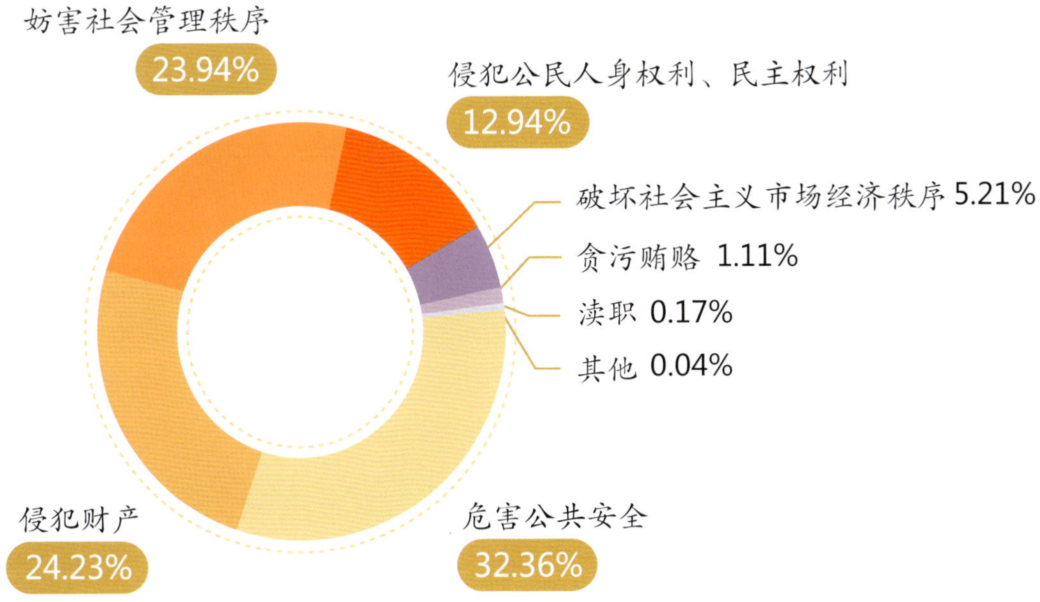

注："其他"包括危害国家安全、危害国防利益等案件。

7 2019年排名前十的一审刑事案件

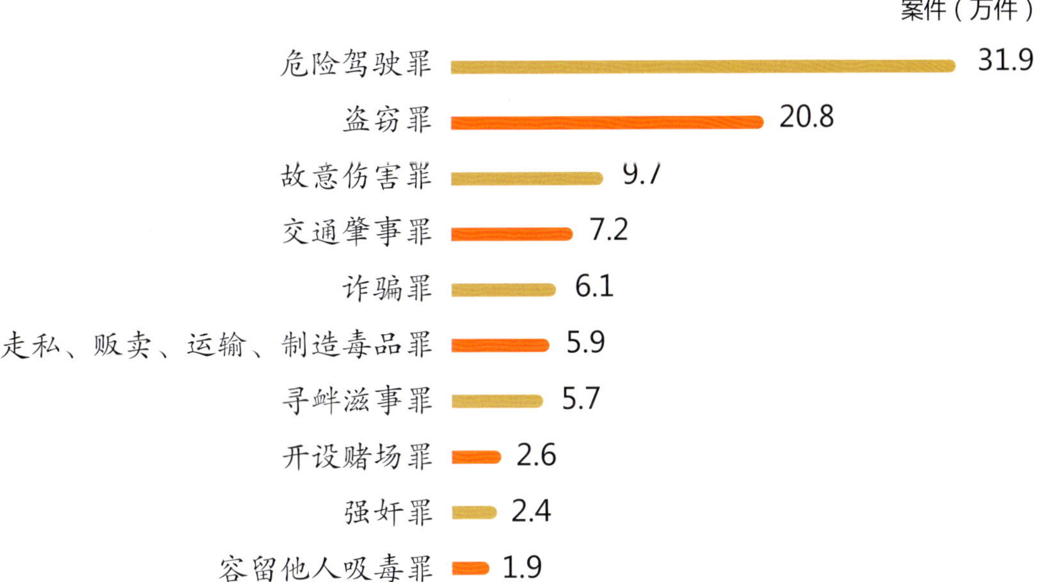

8 2019年一审民商事案件构成

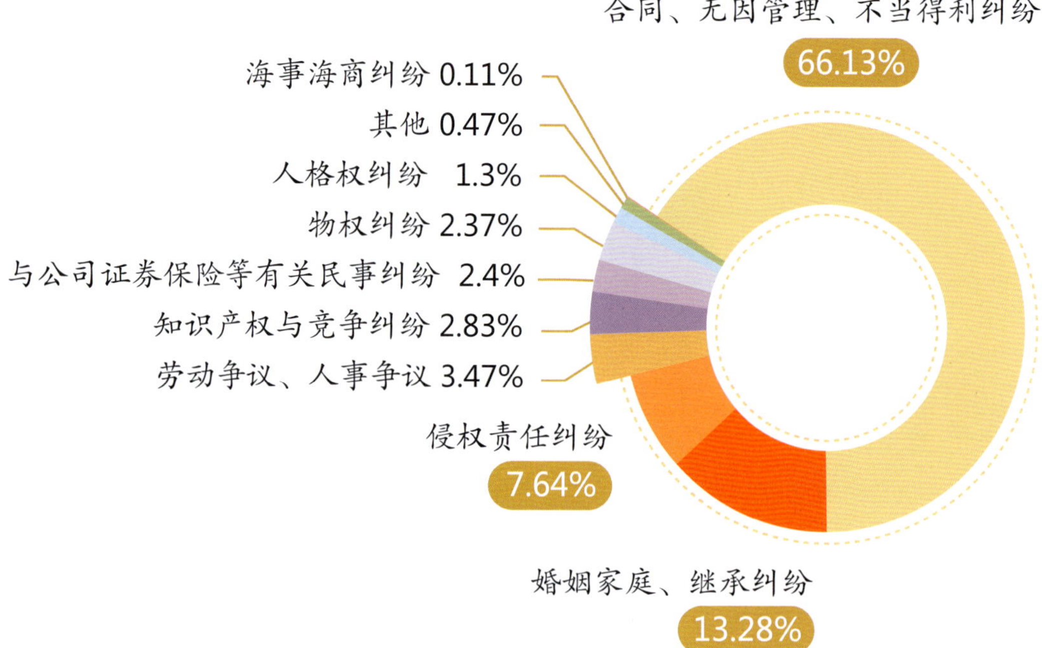

注：“其他”为适用特殊程序案件。

9 2019年部分一审民商事案件增长情况

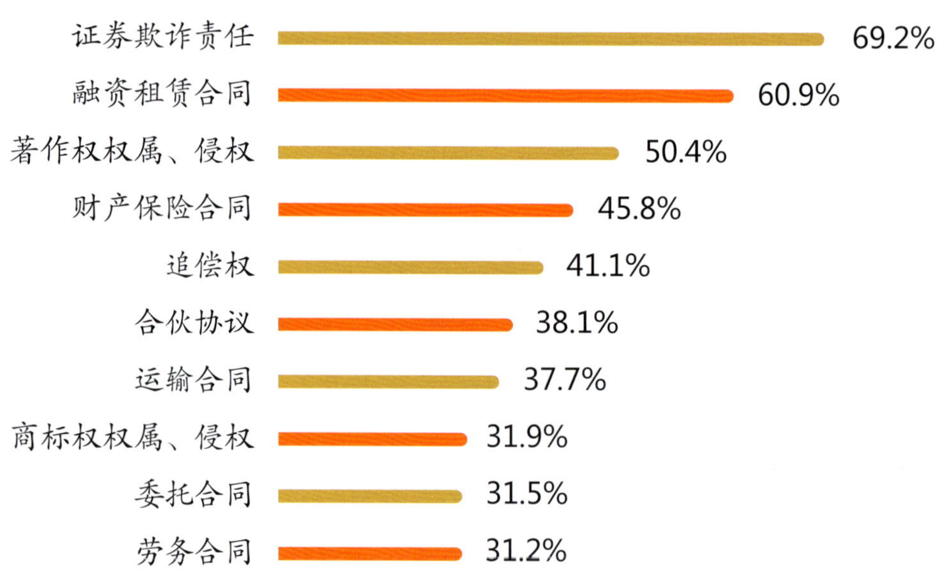

10 2019年部分一审行政案件增长情况

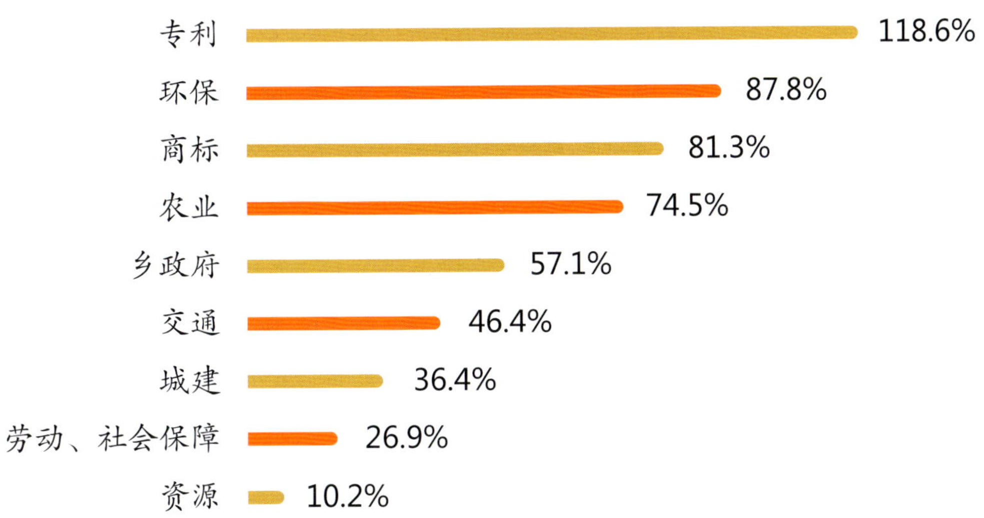

注：上述案件按照行政管理领域进行划分，如专利指专利行政管理领域的行政案件。

11 最高人民法院巡回法庭工作情况

巡回法庭审结案件占最高人民法院审结案件比例情况

巡回法庭妥善处理一批历史形成的跨行政区域重大行政和民商事案件，实现了审判工作重心下移、就地解决纠纷等改革目标，被人民群众称为“家门口的最高人民法院”。

12 涉诉进京访数量

三、推进建设更高水平的平安中国

1 坚决维护国家安全和社会稳定

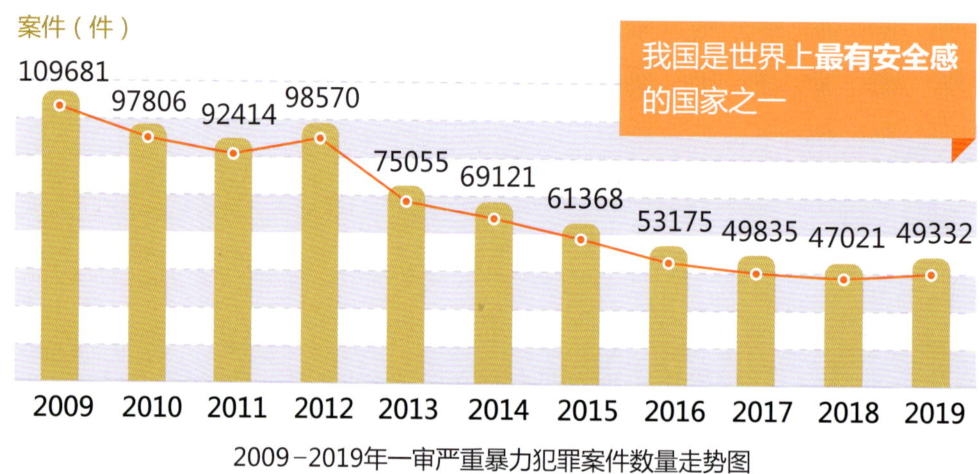

2009－2019年一审严重暴力犯罪案件数量走势图

注：上述统计范围主要涵盖故意杀人罪、强奸罪、抢劫罪、绑架罪、爆炸罪等严重暴力犯罪。

2 依法严惩危害人民群众生命健康和财产安全犯罪

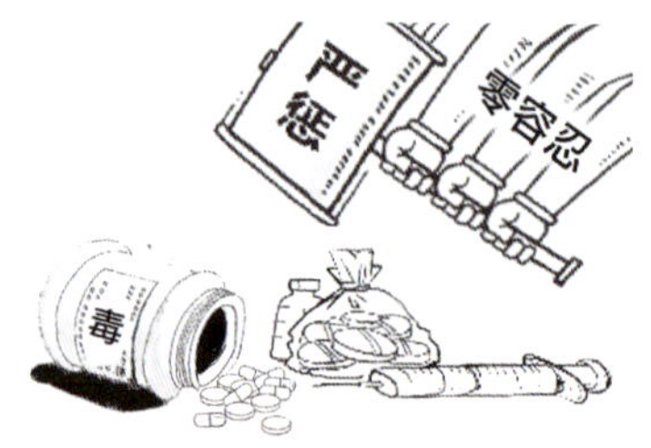

对毒品犯罪“零容忍”

审结毒品犯罪案件**85759**件
重刑率高出同期刑事案件**14.1**个百分点

守好人民群众的“钱袋子”

审结涉众型经济犯罪案件**14899**件
同比上升**21.2**%

严惩电信网络诈骗犯罪

审结电信网络诈骗犯罪案件**7613**件
同比上升**29.3**%

司法守卫
“头顶安全”

保护人民群众“头顶上的安全”

出台审理高空抛物、坠物案件16条意见
依法审理一批高空抛物危害公共安全案件

3 深入开展扫黑除恶专项斗争

涉黑犯罪

一审结案 **1866**件 同比增长**239.3%**

判处罪犯 **22382**人

重刑率达 **55.4%**

涉恶犯罪

一审结案 **10773**件 同比增长**120.4%**

判处罪犯 **61530**人

重刑率达 **26.3%**

典型案例

对孙小果、杜少平等涉黑涉恶犯罪组织头目坚决判处并执行死刑，对黑恶势力犯罪形成有力震慑

孙小果案宣判

制度保障

办理恶势力刑事案件意见

办理“套路贷”刑事案件意见

办理非法放贷刑事案件意见

具体效果

打伞破网

移送涉“保护伞”线索**4843**条 **4313**人

深挖彻查

发现并移送涉黑涉恶线索**25049**条 **30802**人

综合治理

为社会治安防控体系完善发出**7865**条司法建议

打财断血

对涉黑犯罪罪犯、恶势力犯罪集团成员、恶势力团伙成员判处财产刑人数比例为**95.9%**、**63.9%**、**52.7%**分别高出同期全部刑事案件**50.7**、**18.7**、**7.5**个百分点

专项斗争开展以来，共判处没收全部财产**1767**人，判处罚金、没收部分财产**100.9亿**元

四、依法服务经济社会持续健康发展

1 营造稳定公平透明、可预期的法治化营商环境

近三年我国营商环境世界排名情况

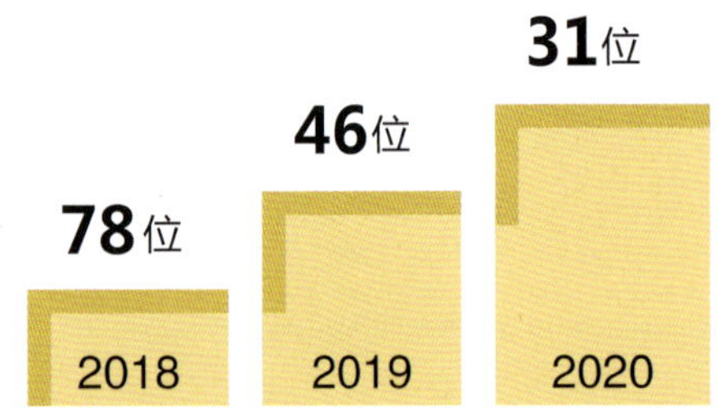

法治是最好的营商环境

连续2年

跻身全球优化营商环境
改善幅度最大的十大经济体

注：以上数据源于世界银行每年发布的营商环境报告。

司法助力优化营商环境

2019年司法解释与部分规范性文件

“执行合同”指标排名：第5位

评价民商事司法制度与法院工作质效

- 严格规范民商事案件延长审限和延期开庭
- 加大民商事案件平均审理天数、结案率等信息公开力度

“司法程序质量”指标

全球第1

被世界银行评价为

全球最佳实践者

“办理破产”指标排名：第51位

评价市场救治退出机制与质效

- 出台破产法司法解释（三）
- 北京、上海、深圳等地设立破产法庭

“保护中小投资者”指标排名：第28位

评价在投资者发生利益冲突时法律对中小投资者保护力度

- 出台公司法司法解释（五）

2 服务高质量发展

司法助力金融发展

- 12条举措 • 出台为推动经济高质量发展提供司法服务和保障的意见
- 17条举措 • 出台为设立科创板并试点注册制改革提供司法保障的意见
- 明确12类问题法律适用 • 发布民商事审判工作会议纪要

3 服务打好三大攻坚战

防范化解重大风险攻坚战

★出台办理操纵证券期货市场、利用未公开信息交易等案件司法解释

★全面推进金融纠纷多元化解机制建设

★健全债券纠纷法治化处置机制

上海金融法院

★创新证券纠纷示范判决机制

★建立大宗股票执行协作机制

脱贫攻坚战

★深入实施服务乡村振兴战略45条意见

★严惩涉农骗补骗保、基层腐败犯罪

★发布“农资打假”典型案例

污染防治攻坚战

★制定审理生态环境损害赔偿案件司法解释

★成立南京、兰州环境资源法庭

★建立长江、黄河、大运河环境资源司法协作机制

长江经济带生态环境司法保护典型案例

4 加强产权司法保护

民营企业家座谈会

废止103件司法解释

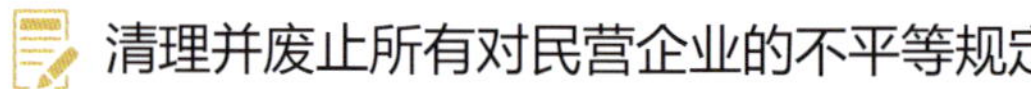
清理并废止所有对民营企业的不平等规定

严格区分

	≠	
经济纠纷		经济犯罪
民事责任		刑事责任
合法财产		违法所得
公司财产		个人财产
正当融资		非法集资

5 服务创新驱动发展

知产法庭成绩单

加快知识产权专业化审判组织体系建设

最高人民法院知识产权法庭
（审理全国范围内专利等专业技术性较强的知识产权上诉案件）

★促进统一技术类知识产权案件裁判标准

★建立全国法院技术调查资源统筹共享机制

北京、上海、广州知识产权法院

各地设立21个知识产权法庭

6 服务更高水平对外开放

服务共建“一带一路”

★出台外商投资法司法解释

★出台进一步为“一带一路”建设提供司法服务和保障的意见

★推进最高人民法院国际商事法庭实质化运行

服务自贸试验区和自由贸易港建设

★出台为中国（上海）自贸试验区临港新片区建设提供司法服务和保障的意见

★设立海南第一、第二涉外民商事法庭

★建立域外法查明平台

五、依法保障社会公平正义和人民权利

1 大力弘扬社会主义核心价值观

弘扬正气正义

严惩侮辱国旗国徽国歌犯罪

国家象征庄严神圣不可侵犯

木里救火牺牲英烈案

英烈精神不容亵渎

撞伤儿童离开遇阻猝死案

鼓励公众见义勇为

网络众筹退款案

保障网络公益健康发展

2 努力提高人民群众获得感幸福感安全感

反家暴
签发人身安全保护令**2004**份

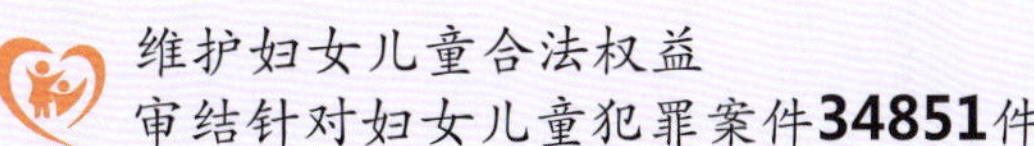

维护妇女儿童合法权益
审结针对妇女儿童犯罪案件**34851**件

护薪行动
追讨农民工“血汗钱”**107亿**元

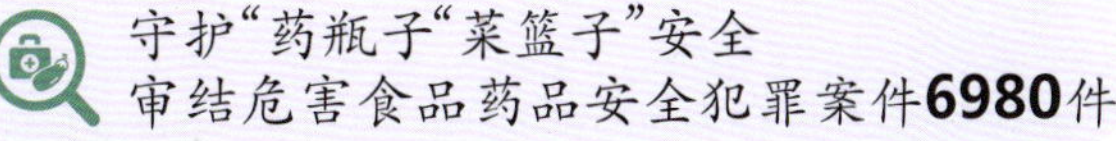

守护“药瓶子”“菜篮子”安全
审结危害食品药品安全犯罪案件**6980**件

3 保护少年儿童健康成长

对罪行极其严重的性侵儿童犯罪分子

★ 依法判处死刑

惩治校园欺凌

★ 审结校园欺凌和校园暴力案件**4192**件

保护儿童合法权益

★ 审结抚养费案件**58734**件

法治教育从娃娃抓起

★ 青少年法治教育漫画绘本丛书

六、全面推进一站式多元解纷和诉讼服务体系建设

1 制度设计

《最高人民法院关于建设一站式多元解纷机制一站式诉讼服务中心的意见》

到2020年底

- 一站式多元解纷机制基本健全
- 一站式诉讼服务中心全面建成
- 普遍开通网上立案功能
- 全面推行跨域立案服务

《最高人民法院关于建设一站式多元解纷机制一站式诉讼服务中心的意见》

2 一站式多元解纷机制运行效果

- 全国四成法院实现以10%的法官化解40%以上民商事案件目标
- 审理周期缩短近一半
- 服判息诉率明显提高

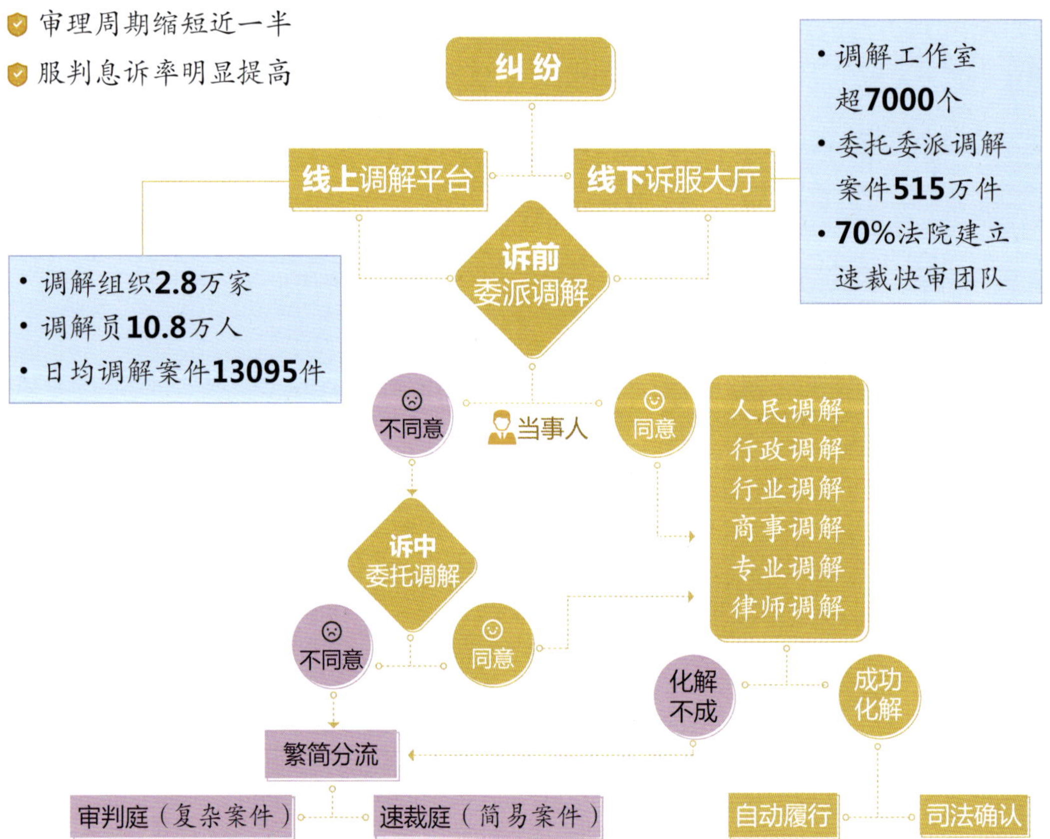

3 一站式诉讼服务中心集成建设效果

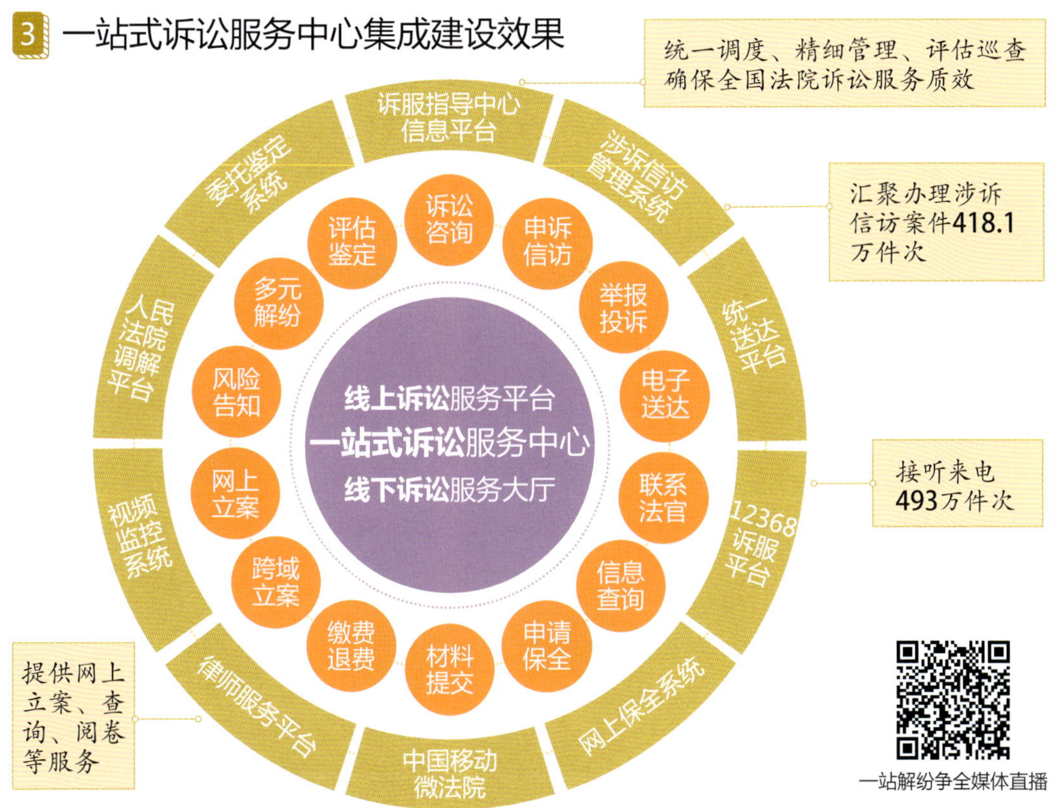

4 跨域立案诉讼服务

跨域立案2.7万件，其中省级行政区内跨域立案2.1万件，跨省级行政区立案6452件

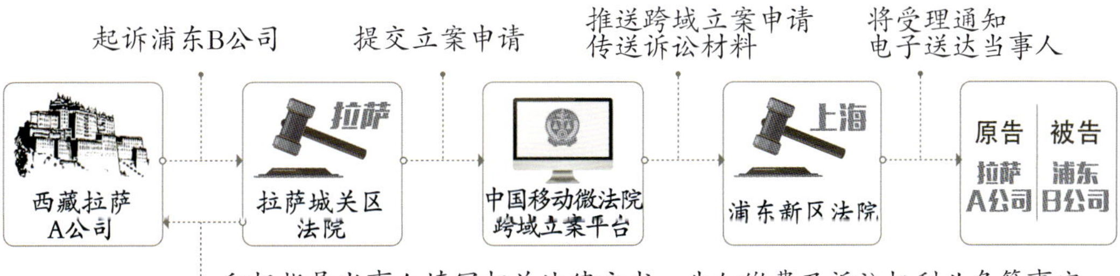

内蒙古法院创新跨域诉讼服务

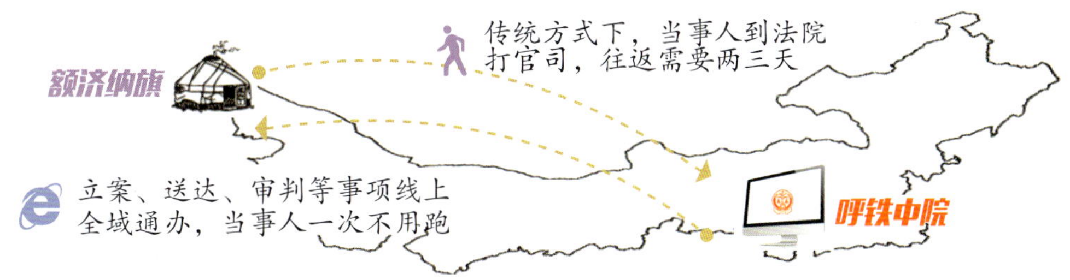

七、巩固“基本解决执行难”成果

贯彻中央全面依法治国委员会《关于加强综合治理从源头切实解决执行难问题的意见》

发布实施人民法院执行工作纲要（2019-2023）

出台善意文明执行和律师参与执行意见

配合民事强制执行立法

开展“巩固基本解决执行难工作成果”专项执行行动

加大“五类案件”执行力度

- 涉黑恶势力犯罪
- 涉职务犯罪
- 涉民生
- 涉金融债权和金融犯罪
- 涉基层党政机关和国企拖欠民营企业债务

加强三项重点管理工作

- “一案双查”制度
- “一案一账号”案款管理机制
- 智慧执行建设

“3+1”核心指标继续保持高水平运行

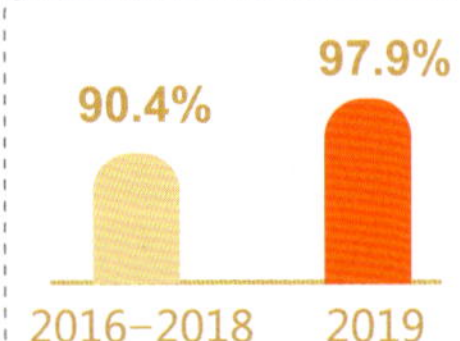

全国法院有财产可供执行案件法定期限内执结率

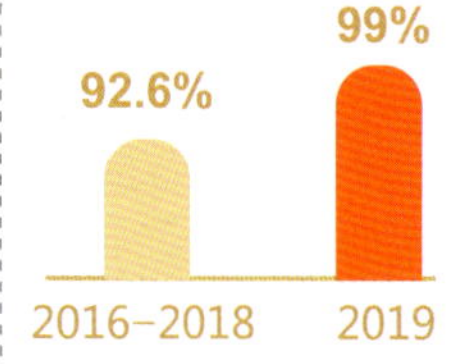

全国法院无财产可供执行案件终结本次执行程序合格率

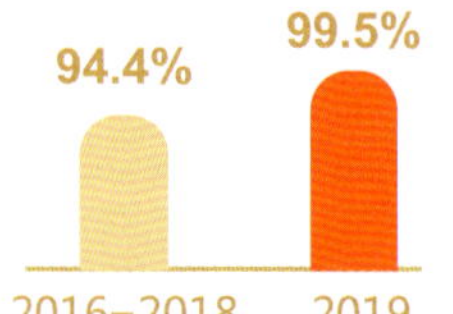

全国法院执行信访案件办结率

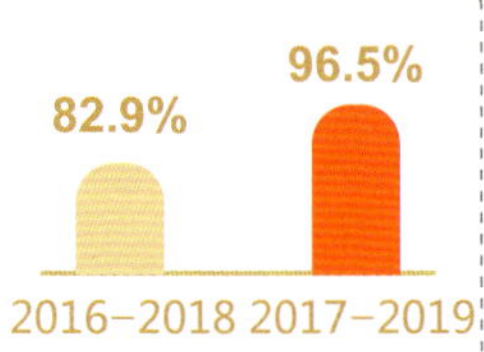

近三年执行案件整体执结率

八、深化司法体制综合配套改革

制定实施人民法院第五个五年改革纲要

健全审判权力运行监督制约机制

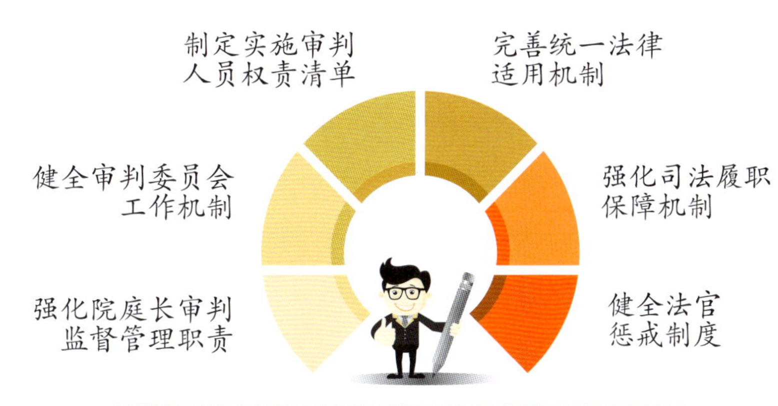

放权不放任 用权受监督

开展民事诉讼程序繁简分流改革试点

推进案件繁简分流、轻重分离、快慢分道

深入推进以审判为中心的刑事诉讼制度改革

- 坚持罪刑法定、疑罪从无、证据裁判 → 依法宣告**1388**名被告人无罪
- 认真落实认罪认罚从宽制度 → 出台关于适用认罪认罚从宽制度指导意见

九、全面建设智慧法院

智慧法院实验室

 党的十八大以来智慧法院建设重要节点

2019

- 12月 “全国智慧法院关键技术及重大应用”科技成果被中国电子学会鉴定认为总体达到国际领先水平
- 12月 最高人民法院智慧法院实验室启用
- 12月 全国中级、基层法院全面实现跨域立案服务
- 11月 人民法庭工作平台、人民法庭信息平台上线
- 6月 建成诉讼服务指导中心信息平台
- 5月 建成全国统一司法区块链平台
- 3月 建设推广移动微法院

2018

- 设立北京、广州互联网法院 9月
- 人民法院大数据管理和服务平台获评数字中国建设年度最佳实践 4月
- 人民法院调解平台上线 2月

2017

- 11月 推广道路交通纠纷“网上数据一体化处理”平台
- 8月 设立杭州互联网法院

2016

- 全国法院实现“一张网”办公办案 11月
- 开通中国庭审公开网 9月
- 开通全国企业破产重整案件信息网 8月
- 开展电子卷宗随案同步生成 7月
- “法信”上线 3月

2015

- 12月 开通最高人民法院律师服务平台
- 2月 开通全国法院减刑、假释、暂予监外执行信息网

2014

- 开通中国审判流程信息公开网 开通中国执行信息公开网 11月
- 开通网上申诉信访平台 2月

2013

- 7月 开通中国裁判文书网

扫码看庭审

司法大数据成果展示

2 探索互联网司法新模式

网络空间治理法治化“试验田”：互联网法院

北京互联网法院

杭州互联网法院

广州互联网法院

在线审结案件**97196**件

在线庭审平均用时**26**分钟

平均审理周期**42**天

中国移动微法院

一键体验移动微法院

实名用户**87万**人

办理网上立案**121万**件

网上送达文书**400万**份

全国统一司法区块链平台

已上链存证固证**3.27亿**条

2019年12月5日，最高人民法院在浙江乌镇举办世界互联网法治论坛，25个国家和地区代表出席并通过《乌镇宣言》，推动构建互联互通、共享共治的网络空间命运共同体。

3 阳光司法机制更趋成熟定型

中国裁判文书网

公布文书

9195万份

中国庭审公开网

直播案件**696万**件

全球最大政务视频直播网站

中国审判流程信息公开网

向当事人公开案件

2900万件

信息**15.24亿**项

中国执行信息公开网

向当事人全面公开

执行案件信息

十、人民法院队伍建设

英雄模范 新时代司法为民、公正司法的先进典型

法治人物-李庆军

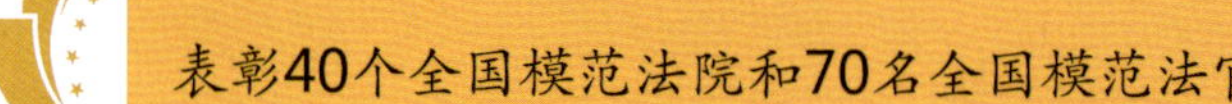
表彰40个全国模范法院和70名全国模范法官

法治人物-赵鑫

李庆军：全国模范法官

赵　鑫：全国“人民满意

的公务员”

表彰全国法院“基本解决执行难”工作100个先进单位和100名先进个人，深切缅怀攻坚战中牺牲的51名干警

人才培养 大力加强高素质专业化人才建设

走进中国政法实务大讲堂

- 全国法院教育培训规划（2019–2023）
- 挂职和研修学者累计70人 法律实习生累计412人
- 2019年最高人民法院接收安置军队转业干部20人
- 最高人民法院云课堂
- 培养评定双语法官1345人
- 省级审判业务专家1329人

正风肃纪 2015–2019年人民法院查处违纪违法人员情况

最高人民法院查处违纪违法干警人数

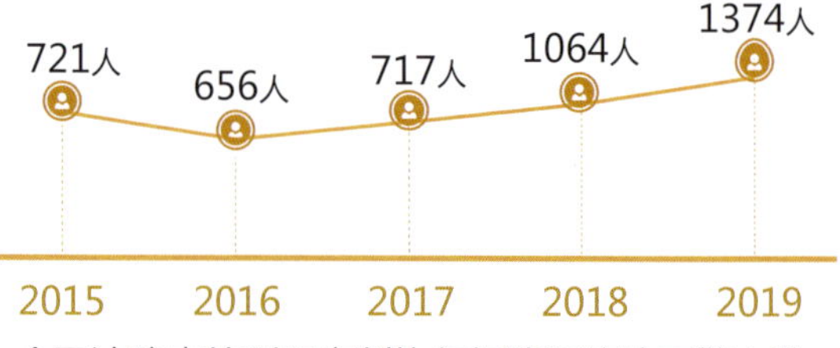

全国法院查处利用审判执行权违纪违法干警人数

中国法院博物馆被中宣部命名为全国爱国主义教育示范基地

电影《马锡五断案》：“一刻也不离开群众”
（一刻也不离开群众）

为庆祝新中国成立70周年
评选“献给祖国的公平正义之歌”优秀原创歌曲

《诺言》

多少心底的呼唤
多少期待的双眼
我们用公正的诺言
把温暖贴近你胸前
曾无数不眠的夜晚
写下天平的箴言
纵然我一生平凡
也要捍卫法的尊严

《溜索法官》

溜索牵两岸
溜索两岸牵
多少故事流淌在岁月的长河边
公平牵两岸
公平两岸牵
多少温情长留在山水一线

微视频《绽放》
背着国徽去审判

《法官誓言》

一种执着存在心间
要守护在天平两端
乘风破浪有何不敢
在平凡的日子里灿烂

献给祖国的
公平正义之歌

《宁海路75号》

世界很大 我们很小
谁年少不向往天涯海角
梦想易逝 红颜易老
每天在现实里移动双脚
昼夜奔跑 此中味道
早在你心上烙下记号

十一、全国人大代表建议、全国政协提案落实情况

1 2019年代表建议、政协提案办理情况

代表建议 355件
日常建议 395件

政协提案173件

建议提案分布情况

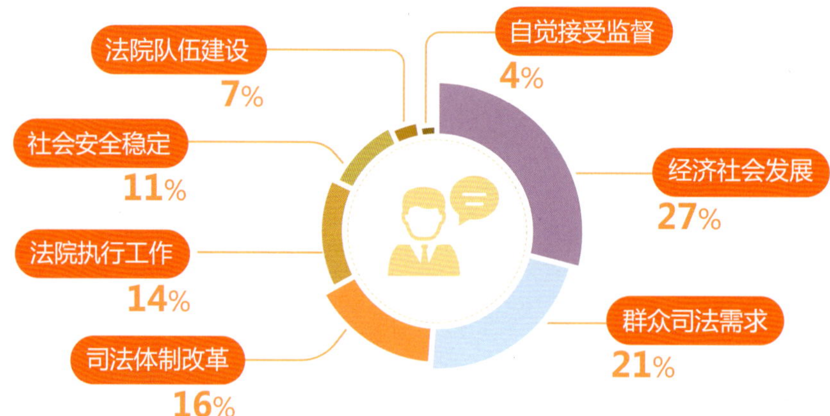

2 代表、委员联络工作情况

代表联络工作

委员联络工作

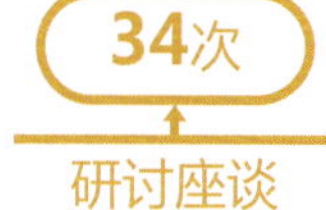

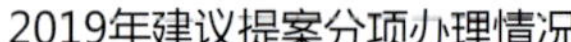

2019年建议提案分项办理情况

2019年建议提案详细落实情况

2019年建议提案公开复文情况

3 2019年代表建议、政协提案落实情况

序号	代表建议、政协提案主要内容	有关落实情况
1	深化司法体制综合配套改革	出台人民法院第五个五年改革纲要（2019–2023）。
2	进一步全面落实司法责任制	出台《关于健全完善人民法院审判委员会工作机制的意见》，制定审判人员权力清单和责任清单，发布建立法律适用分歧解决机制实施办法。
3	平等保护民营企业	发布《关于废止部分司法解释（第十三批）的决定》，废止103件司法解释，废除所有对民营企业的不平等规定。
4	全面建设现代化诉讼服务体系	出台《关于建设一站式多元解纷机制 一站式诉讼服务中心的意见》，推进一站式多元解纷和诉讼服务机制建设。
5	依法惩治腐败犯罪	指导审理包括“百名红通”人员在内的多起腐败犯罪案件，不断完善职务犯罪案件审判工作机制。
6	严惩黑恶势力犯罪	会同有关部门出台《关于办理恶势力刑事案件若干问题的意见》《关于办理实施“软暴力”的刑事案件若干问题的意见》等规范性文件，深入推进扫黑除恶专项斗争。
7	严厉打击“套路贷”“校园贷”犯罪	会同有关部门出台《关于办理“套路贷”刑事案件若干问题的意见》《关于办理非法放贷刑事案件若干问题的意见》等规范性文件。
8	严惩新型网络犯罪	会同有关部门出台《关于办理非法利用信息网络、帮助信息网络犯罪活动等刑事案件适用法律若干问题的解释》。
9	加强对电信网络诈骗案件审判指导	发布10件电信网络诈骗犯罪典型案例。
10	加强未成年人权益保护	发布保护未成年人权益十大优秀案例和强奸、猥亵儿童犯罪典型案例，编写青少年法治教育丛书。
11	加强民生司法保障	出台《人民法院国家司法救助案件办理程序规定（试行）》，下发《关于进一步加强拖欠农民工工资案件审判执行工作的通知》，会同有关部门下发《关于进一步加强合作建立健全妇女儿童权益保护工作机制的通知》，发布司法救助典型案例。
12	服务经济高质量发展	出台《关于为推动经济高质量发展提供司法服务和保障的意见》。
13	服务保障“三大攻坚战”	出台《关于为防范化解重大风险提供司法服务和保障的意见》，出台办理操纵证券期货市场、利用未公开信息交易、非法集资、非法买卖外汇等案件司法解释和规范性文件；深入实施服务乡村振兴战略45条意见，发布“农资打假”典型案例；出台《关于审理生态环境损害赔偿案件的若干规定（试行）》，成立南京、兰州环境资源法庭。

14	服务科创板改革创新	出台《关于为设立科创板并试点注册制改革提供司法保障的若干意见》。
15	完善多元化纠纷解决机制	单独或会同有关部门出台进一步完善委派调解机制、深入开展价格争议纠纷调解工作以及全面推进金融纠纷多元化解机制建设的意见，发布金融纠纷多元化解十大典型案例。
16	加强破产审判工作	出台《关于适用〈中华人民共和国企业破产法〉若干问题的规定（三）》。
17	加强民商事审判工作	出台《全国法院民商事审判工作会议纪要》《关于适用〈中华人民共和国公司法〉若干问题的规定（五）》《关于修改〈关于民事诉讼证据的若干规定〉的决定》。
18	加强行政审判工作	出台《关于审理行政协议案件若干问题的规定》。
19	加强知识产权审判工作	成立海口、厦门知识产权法庭，发布2018年中国法院知识产权司法保护10大案件和50件典型案件，出台《关于技术调查官参与知识产权案件诉讼活动的若干规定》。
20	服务“一带一路”建设	出台《关于人民法院进一步为“一带一路”建设提供司法服务和保障的意见》《关于适用〈中华人民共和国外商投资法〉若干问题的解释》，设立南京海事法院。
21	服务粤港澳大湾区建设	出台有关为粤港澳大湾区建设提供司法服务和保障的文件。
22	全面推进智慧法院建设	编印人民法院信息化建设五年发展规划，发布人民法院信息化标准；各级法院基本建成科技法庭和远程视频庭审系统；31个高级法院和新疆兵团分院全部接入中国移动微法院。
23	加强公益诉讼制度建设	会同有关部门发布《关于人民检察院提起刑事附带民事公益诉讼应否履行诉前公告程序问题的批复》，在人民法院公告网开通专栏，集中免费刊登公益诉讼案件公告。
24	健全执行工作长效机制	出台深化执行改革健全解决执行难长效机制、在执行工作中进一步强化善意文明执行理念以及深入推进律师参与人民法院执行工作等意见。
25	深化认罪认罚从宽制度改革	会同有关部门出台《关于适用认罪认罚从宽制度的指导意见》。
26	加强人民陪审员管理	出台《关于适用〈中华人民共和国人民陪审员法〉若干问题的解释》，会同有关部门出台《人民陪审员培训、考核、奖惩工作办法》。
27	完善员额法官退出机制	出台《人民法院法官员额退出办法（试行）》。
28	建立科学的员额法官动态调整机制	出台《省级以下人民法院法官员额动态调整指导意见（试行）》。

附件二

2020年人民法院工作要点

报告所涉部分用语和案例

（仅供参考）

1.审结、执结2902.2万件：指地方各级人民法院2019年审结、执结各类案件总数。其中，审结刑事案件1975511件，占6.81%；民商事案件16177373件，占55.74%；行政案件692034件，占2.38%；国家赔偿与司法救助案件57377件，占0.20%；执结执行案件9546952件，占32.90%；强制清算与破产案件17399件，占0.06%；其他案件555710件，占1.91%。报告中的案件数据，未经特别说明的，均为一审结案数据。报告中反映的各项工作，包括最高人民法院和地方各级人民法院工作。

2.民族资产解冻类电信网络诈骗：指犯罪分子利用群众对党和政府的信任，围绕国家大政方针和社会热点，编造民族大业、精准扶贫、“一带一路”、军民融合、慈善帮扶等各种民族资产类虚假项目，以交纳少量启动费用便可获得巨额回报为名实施的诈骗犯罪。该类犯罪通过微信等互联网途径层层发展下线，裂变式传播，受骗人数众多，涉案金额巨大。

3.张志超案：2006年3月，张志超被以强奸罪判处无期徒刑，剥夺政治权利终身。2017年11月，最高人民法院作出再审决定，认为原审判决认定事实不清，主要证据之间存在矛盾，指令山东高院再审。2020年1月，山东高院再审宣告张志超无罪。该案体现了人民法院坚持实事求是、有错必纠，对错案发现一起、纠正一起的鲜明态度。

4. 范太应案：2014年12月，陕西延安中院对范太应故意杀人案作出无罪判决后，检察机关提出抗诉，附带民事诉讼原告人提出上诉。陕西高院裁定驳回抗诉、上诉，维持无罪判决。该案审理过程中，人民法院坚持以事实为根据、以法律为准绳，坚决落实疑罪从无原则，严格贯彻证据裁判规则，认真审查案件事实证据，依法作出判决，坚决守住防范冤错案件的底线，充分体现了坚守司法良知、坚持原则底线的担当精神，也体现出推进以审判为中心的刑事诉讼制度改革的重大意义。

5. 倪菊葆案：2010年3月，倪菊葆因在担任4家单位法定代表人期间实施变相非法吸收公众存款等行为，被以非法吸收公众存款罪、合同诈骗罪判处有期徒刑二十年，并处罚金80万元。2018年11月，倪菊葆以其不构成合同诈骗罪为由提出申诉。2019年7月，江苏苏州中院再审认为倪菊葆实施的拆借资金行为不构成合同诈骗罪，该部分犯罪数额应计入非法吸收公众存款数额，遂以非法吸收公众存款罪改判倪菊葆有期徒刑九年，并处罚金40万元。该案依法改判，体现了人民法院依法甄别纠正历史形成的涉产权冤错案件的鲜明态度，对于稳定民营企业家预期，营造法治化营商环境，保障民营企业家安心干事创业具有重要意义。

6.“泛亚有色”案：泛亚公司董事长单某某与主管人员郭某等经商议策划，违反金融管理法律规定，以稀有金属买卖融资融货为名推行“委托交割受托申报”“委托受托”等业务，诱使社会公众投资，变相吸收巨额公众存款，给集资参与人造成巨额经济损失。云南法院以非法吸收公众存款罪对泛亚公司判处罚金10亿元；以非法吸收公众存款罪、职务侵占罪判处单某某有期徒刑十八年，并处没收个人财产5000万元，罚金50万元；对郭某等20人判处相应刑罚。

7. 通过暗管向长江违法排放有毒物质污染环境案：2007年起，亚兰德公司埋设暗管将生产污水直接排放到长江，并通过操控暗管阀门、冲洗车间等手段逃避环保检查，违法排污状况持续10年，违规排放废水48万多吨，造成生态环境损害数额量化结果高达750余万元。安徽芜湖法院综合犯罪情况及其社会危害程度，分别对亚兰德公司及相关人员以污染环境罪追究刑事责任，要求该公司支付相应生态环境修复费用。本案判决明确，实施污染环境犯罪的排污企业在承担生态环境修复费用后仍需承担刑事责任，单位犯罪中直接负责人员亦需承担刑事责任，彰显从严惩治污染环境犯罪的决心，有力威慑违法排污单位并对相关从业人员具有教育警示作用。

8. 撞伤儿童离开遇阻猝死案：郭某某骑自行车与5岁的罗某某相撞，造成罗右颌受伤出血、倒在地上。孙某见状阻止意欲离开的郭某某，并与其发生争执。郭某某情绪激动，被物业公司保安劝阻后坐在石墩上，不久因心脏骤停死亡。郭某某家属将孙某及物业公司诉至法院。河南信阳法院审理认为，孙某阻拦郭某某的方式和内容均在正常限度内，对郭死亡后果的发生没有过错，且行为目的是保护儿童利益，不存在侵害郭的故意或过失，不承担侵权责任；保安的履职行为与郭的死亡亦无因果关系，判决驳回原告诉讼请求。该案判决明确是非对错，提供行为指引，弘扬社会正气，有利于鼓励公众见义勇为。

9. 患者飞踹医生反被伤案： 一患者因到诊所结算欠款时未带现金而与医生发生争吵，被劝离后再度返回诊所并欲飞踹医生，被医生侧身躲过并抓腿掀倒，致左腿骨折。河南驻马店中院审理认为，医生的行为属正当防卫，判决医生无罪，且不承担民事赔偿责任。该案判决旗帜鲜明向“谁受伤谁有理”的“和稀泥”做法说不，有力维护了医务人员正当防卫的权利。

10. 微信群主踢群第一案： 柳某某因违反微信群公告被群主刘某某移出群组后，以刘侵犯其名誉权为由诉至法院。山东青岛法院审理认为，微信群主行使平台设置的管理权限是互联网群组内“谁建群谁负责”“谁管理谁负责”自治规则的运用，本案中刘某某并未对柳某某进行负面评价，柳基于被刘移出群组行为提起的侵权诉讼不属于法院受案范围，其提起诉讼缺乏正当性，遂裁定驳回起诉，案件受理费不予退还。该案进一步明确了互联网群组自治规则，有利于引导公众自觉遵守互联网群组管理有关规定，通过合理方式解决纠纷，防止权利滥用。

11. 群众说事、民事直说、法官说法： 陕西延安富县在村组设立“说事室”和“一村（社区）一法官”，由乡村干部通过“拉家常、讲政策、讲道理”的方式先行化解矛盾纠纷，实现群众自我管理。当“群众说事”涉及专业法律问题时，由法官及时进行说法答疑，引导群众运用法治思维和法治方式化解矛盾纠纷。甘肃两当县坚持“有事坐在一起好好说”，搭建“民事直说”平台，召集群众当面反映问题，集中力量现场办理，与法院多元解纷机制对接，把矛盾化解在基层。群众说事、民事直说、法官说法把党的领导与群众自治、政府管理与群众自我管理、依法治县与以德治村相结合，充分体现了党的领导、人民当家作主、依法治国的有机统一。

12.“暗刷流量”案：常某某、许某约定通过“暗刷流量”为某软件产品增加访问量，后因费用支付问题发生争议而诉至法院。北京互联网法院审理认为，“暗刷流量”属欺诈性点击行为，双方订立的合同违背公序良俗、损害社会公共利益，属于无效合同，双方当事人不得基于该合同获利，遂判决驳回原告诉讼请求，收缴双方的非法获利。

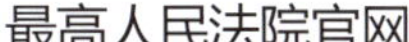

最高人民法院官网

最高人民法院微信公众号

最高人民法院微博

Report on the Work of the Supreme People's Court of the People's Republic of China*

Delivered at the Third Session of the 13th National People's Congress on May 25, 2020

By Zhou Qiang, President of the Supreme People's Court

Fellow Deputies,

On behalf of the Supreme People's Court (SPC), I now present to you the report on the work of the SPC for your deliberation, and I welcome comments on my report from the members of the National Committee of the Chinese People's Political Consultative Conference (CPPCC).

Since the coronavirus first emerged, General Secretary Xi Jinping has personally taken charge and planned our response. The Communist Party Central Committee with Comrade Xi Jinping at its core rallied the Party, the armed forces, and the

* In the event of any inconsistency between the Chinese and English versions, the Chinese version shall prevail.

people of all ethnic groups in China and led them in surmounting difficulties. Through hard work, we have achieved a decisive victory in the battle to defend Hubei Province and its capital city Wuhan, made major strategic achievements in our response to the epidemic, and produced progress in advancing epidemic control while promoting economic and social development. The major achievements we have achieved are essentially owed to the strong leadership of the Party Central Committee with Comrade Xi Jinping at its core, which fully shows the superiority of socialist system under the leadership of the Communist Party of China (CPC), and demonstrates China's strength, spirit and efficiency to the world.

The SPC resolutely implements General Secretary Xi Jinping's important instructions and the Party Central Committee's decisions. Under the leadership of the Committee of Political and Legal Affairs of the CPC Central Committee, the SPC has acted on the requirements for epidemic prevention and control according to law, and independently or jointly with relevant units formulated opinions on punishment of crimes hindering epidemic prevention and control and crimes disturbing border health and quarantine, and opinions on resuming work and production. The SPC has also improved judicial measures to help ensure stability on the six fronts and security in the six areas, and published 57 typical cases of punishing epidemic-related crimes and helping resumption of work and production, in order to serve the epidemic control and benefit the whole society. The people's courts at various levels have coordinately made efforts to prevent and control the epidemic and maintain stability. They have concluded 2,736 epidemic-related cases and helped resolve disputes from source; they have severely punished crimes of infringing upon the safety and dignity of medical workers to protect "the most beautiful retrogrades" with heavy burden during the anti-epidemic battle; they have continued to be prudent, well-intentioned and civilized in judicial activities, and actively solved difficulties for micro, small and medium-sized enterprises; they have adopted methods of remote case filing, online trials and smart enforcement to timely quell disputes. During the epidemic prevention and control period, the smart courts have played an important role. Throughout the country, in smart courts, there have been 1.36 million cases filed online, 250 thousand court sessions, 590 thousand mediations, 4.46 million electronic services, 2.66 million items of online inquiry and control, 63.9 billion yuan transaction in online judicial auctions, and 204.5 billion yuan enforcement amount. Court cadres, especially those in Hubei and its capital Wuhan, have resolutely responded to the order of the Party Central Committee and actively acted on the anti-epidemic front lines, so as to provide judicial service and guarantee for the overall promotion of epidemic control and economic and social development. They have shown their political nature of staying loyal to the Party, to the nation, to the people and to the law.

Review of Work in 2019

In 2019, the SPC, guided by Xi Jinping Thought on Socialism with Chinese Characteristics for a New Era, under the firm leadership of the CPC Central Committee with Comrade Xi Jinping at its core, and under the effective supervision of the National People's Congress (NPC) and its Standing Committee, strengthened our consciousness of the need to maintain political integrity, think in big-picture terms, follow the leadership core, and keep in alignment with the central Party leadership; stayed confident in the path, theory, system, and culture of socialism with Chinese characteristics; and upheld General Secretary Xi Jinping's core position on the Party Central Committee and in the Party as a whole, and upheld the Party Central Committee's authority and its centralized, unified leadership; fully implemented the guiding principles of the Party's 19th National Congress and the second, third, and fourth plenary sessions of its 19th Central Committee; followed the important speeches when General Secretary Xi Jinping chaired the Politburo Standing Committee meeting and listened to the work report of the SPC Party Group; conscientiously implemented the decisions adopted on the second session of the 13th NPC. The SPC, by closely pursuing its goal of "enabling the people to feel that fairness and justice is served in every case before the courts" and adhering to the principle of "serving the overall interests of the nation, administrating justice for the people and maintaining judicial fairness", fulfilled the duties bestowed by the Constitution and laws faithfully, and made new progress in all aspects, thus providing reliable judicial service and guarantee for social and economic development. During the year, the SPC accepted 38,498 cases and concluded 34,481 cases, up by 10.7% and 8.2% year on year respectively. Meanwhile, we also issued 20 judicial interpretations and 33 guiding cases to provide better supervision and guidance to the court trials across the country. Local people's courts at various levels accepted 31.567 million cases, concluded and enforced 29.022 million cases, and the closed cases amounted to a value of 6.6 trillion yuan, up by 12.7%, 15.3% and 20.3% year on year respectively.

I. We fully implemented the overall national security outlook to build a safe China at a higher level

Resolutely safeguarded national security and social stability. People's courts concluded 1.297 million criminal cases of first instance, and convicted 1.66 million criminals. We severely punished crimes of immersion, subversion, destruction, violence, terror, ethnic division and religious extremism in accordance with the law, and firmly defended national political security and the fundamental interests of our people. We always maintained high pressure upon serious crimes against public security. We concluded 49 thousand cases of serious violence, 272 thousand cases of frequent property-related crime, 65 thousand cases involving guns, explosives, gambling and pornography. The number of serious violent crimes declined for ten years successively, and social security remained stable and orderly. We intensified the fight against drugs and concluded 86 thousand drug-related criminal cases. In cooperation with the Ministry of Emergency Management, we strengthened the connection between administrative law enforcement and criminal justice and punished crimes of production safety violations in accordance with the law, in order to protect people's health and property. Together with the Supreme People's Procuratorate and the Ministry of Public Security, we issued opinions on punishment of crimes assaulting police with an aim to effectively safeguard the police's personal safety and law enforcement authority. We also tried a series of major vicious cases according to law such as hijacking a bus to hit people, stabbing innocent people at a school gate and killing passengers during ride sharing. Criminals with extremely serious crimes were sentenced to death pursuant to the law, which could adequately play the deterrent role of the criminal penalty.

Cracked down on organized gang-related crimes. Under the principle of severe punishment according to law, people's courts nationwide concluded 12,639 gang-related cases involving 83,912 people. We tried the Sun Xiaoguo case and the Du Shaoping case of burying a corpse under the playground in accordance with law. The principal criminals Sun Xiaoguo and Du Shaoping were sentenced and executed to death, so that justice could finally be achieved. The SPC, with other relevant agencies, issued opinions on handling criminal cases of evil forces, "routine loans" and illegal lending, to clarify the policy and legal boundaries and ensure severe and accurate punishment. We aimed to resolutely "break their protective umbrellas and nets" and more severely punished public officials who were involved in the organized crimes. We adopted the approach of "cutting off their financial veins" and comprehensively used means of property penalties, recovering and confiscating illegal income to eliminate the economic base of evil forces. Since the specific fight of cracking down on organized crimes, we have punished a group of "sandstone-selling gangsters", "road gangsters", "market gangsters" and "village gangsters", and thus purified the social atmosphere.

Maintained high pressure on punishing corruption crimes. People's courts concluded 25 thousand cases of corruption, bribery and malfeasance with 29 thousand people involved, among which 27 defendants were originally cadres whose appointment was recorded in the Organization Department of the CPC Central Committee. Our trials accurately put into practice the criminal policy of tempering justice with mercy. Defendants like Ai Wenli who voluntarily surrendered to court were treated with leniency according to the law; seriously corrupt officials like

Xing Yun were sentenced to life imprisonment. We improved the linkage mechanism between national supervision and criminal justice with the National Supervisory Commission. We provided active support in extraditing or repatriating the fugitives and illicit money, and concluded 321 cases of corrupted fugitives returning to China for trial. We confiscated the illegal income transferred to overseas by Peng Xufeng and others. We never allowed corrupts to remain at large and escape with impunity.

Enhanced people's sense of safety. We severely punished crimes that endangered food and drug safety, handled major cases like the Changsheng vaccine case and the Xiao Pinghui case of producing and selling water-injected beef according to law, and punished criminal activities such as selling illegally recycled waste cooking oil according to law, in order to ensure food and drug safety for our people. People's courts in Hebei, Shanghai, Jiangsu and other jurisdictions tried criminal cases involving unauthorized imports of generic drugs in accordance with the law, and accurately defined the boundary between crime and innocence, so that both penalty and humanity could coexist in justice. In response to the high incidence of telecommunications and network frauds of national asset unfreezing, the SPC and the Ministry of Public Security issued opinions to apply a more severe punishment. We severely punished "campus loans" crimes so as to protect students' legitimate rights. We strictly punished violence against doctors. We sentenced and executed death to criminals including Sun Wenbin who killed a doctor of Beijing Civil Aviation General Hospital, to protect medical staff's physical safety and legitimate rights and safeguard normal medical order. In terms of falling objects from high that threatened people's safety, we introduced a judicial policy to strengthen punishment in accordance with the law and prevention at the source; we publicly tried a number of relevant cases to protect the safety of people over the head.

The amnesty was granted according to law. We earnestly followed President Xi Jinping's decision of amnesty and the NPC Standing Committee's decision of amnesty. On the eve of the 70th anniversary of the founding of PRC, 23,593 criminals were granted amnesty according to law, demonstrating benevolence of the Party and the government.

Provided better judicial protection for human rights. We adhered to the fact-based and error-correcting approaches. People's courts at various levels based on the adjudication supervision procedure re-tried 1,774 criminal cases and overruled the previous decisions. People's courts in Shandong and other jurisdictions rectified major wrongful convictions according to law such as the Zhang Zhichao case. We concluded 18 thousand cases applied to China's State Compensation Law and guaranteed the lawful rights and interests of the claimant. Adhering to the principles of no penalty without a law, presumption of innocence and evidence-based adjudication, we declared 637 defendants in public prosecution cases and 751 defendants in private prosecution cases innocent according to law. People's courts in Shaanxi declared Fan Taiying innocent in accordance with the law, avoiding a major wrongful conviction. We implemented the criminal policy of "tempering justice with mercy". Justice and leniency should be applied at a proper level, and crimes should be duly punished. We further advanced the reform of the criminal litigation system centered on trials, and comprehensively and accurately applied the leniency system for confession. Together with the Ministry of Justice, the SPC promoted full coverage of lawyer defense in criminal cases to ensure that lawyers perform their duties according to law.

II.We firmly followed the new development concepts to serve the sustainable and healthy growth of economy and society

Created a law-based business environment within China. Law-based governance guarantees the best business environment. The number of concluded commercial cases of first instance reached 4.537 million in 2019. We formulated opinions on serving high-quality development, issued judicial interpretations of the Company Law and the Bankruptcy Law, and published minutes of civil and commercial trial work meetings, in order to unify the application of laws and judgment standards, and to improve judicial transparency and predictability. We heard administrative litigation cases related to the reform to streamline administration and delegate power, improve regulation, and upgrade services according to law; we supported and supervised the administrative organs to exercise law-based government administration; and we closed 284 thousand first-instance administrative cases, thus promoting the construction of a government under the rule of law and optimizing the soft environment. The World Bank's Doing Business Report 2020 shows that China's business environment has leapt significantly in the global rankings. "Contract enforcement", "bankruptcy", "protection of small and medium-sized investors" and other indicators closely related to the judicature have been significantly raised. Among these, the indicator "quality of judicial procedure" was leading and evaluated as a "Global Best Practice" in this field.

Equally protected all kinds of market subjects' lawful rights and interests according to law. We ensured that all market participants, regardless of state-owned or private, domestic- or foreign-funded, large, medium, small or micro enterprises, were treated equally in legal status, legal application and legal responsibility, and were protected according to law. We dealt with the irregular behavior of private enterprises and entrepreneurs in the past with a developmental perspective. We screened and corrected historical property-related wrongful convictions according to law. The Suzhou Intermediate People's Court retried and rectified the case of Ni Jubao, making sure that every single error was corrected. We reviewed all judicial interpretations since the founding of New China, of which we abolished 103 including all inequitable regulations on private enterprises. We strictly prohibited excessive seizure, distrain or freezing of involved assets; and we innovatively applied compulsory measures like "seizure or distrain while allowing normal operation" to minimize the impact on the business of the enterprise. We strictly distinguished between economic disputes and economic crimes, civil liability and criminal liability, legal property and illegal gains, corporate property and personal property, proper financing and illegal fund-raising. When the facts were unclear or the evidence was insufficient, we resolutely released the defendant and declared him/her innocent. All we did was to protect the entrepreneurs' personal and property safety and to stimulate innovation and motivation.

Improved judicial protection over intellectual property rights (IPR). Protection of IPR is the basic guarantee of the driving force for innovation, and protecting IPR means protecting and promoting innovation. People's courts at various levels concluded 418 thousand IPR cases relating to patents, trademarks and copyrights, in order to help innovation-driven development. The Intellectual Property Court of SPC fairly and efficiently tried cases on appeal involving invention and utility model patent, to promote an improved technology innovative rule of law environment. We fairly tried cases of abuse of the market dominance advantage and unfair competition by e-commerce platforms, to maintain equity in the market. We applied the punitive compensation system to increase the cost of torts. People's courts in Fujian and Guangdong properly tried the patent disputes between Qualcomm and Apple, Huawei and Samsung, prompting the parties to reach a global settlement. The World Intellectual Property Organization specially published judicial cases on IPR in China. China has become the country with the most IPR cases, especially patent cases, and our trial period is among the shortest.

Provided assistance to fending off financial risks. The SPC issued a judicial interpretation to punish crimes of manipulating securities and futures market and insider trading according to law. The SPC, with People's Bank of China, China Banking Regulatory Commission and the China Securities Regulatory Commission, promoted the diversified resolution of financial disputes, and protected the legitimate rights and interests of parties such as investors and financial consumers. We formulated judicial guarantee opinions for the establishment of the Science and Technology Innovation Board and the pilot registration system reform, in order to serve the basic system reform of the capital market. People's courts in Beijing, Shanghai and other jurisdictions orderly promoted the settlement of Internet-related financial cases such as "Ezubao" and participated in the handling of major financial risk-related cases in accordance with the law.

People's courts in Yunnan and other jurisdictions tried cases of illegal fund-raising such as "the Fanya Metal Exchange case", actively recovered and disposed of the property involved, and endeavored to help people recover their losses. The Shanghai Financial Court innovated a model judgment mechanism for securities disputes and explored new paths for small and medium investors seeking judicial protection.

Helped win the battle against poverty. We implemented in detail the judicial policy of helping revitalize rural areas. We severely punished crimes that infringe on the interests of rural masses, related to agricultural subsidy and insurance fraud, corruption in poverty alleviation and agricultural material fraud. People's courts in Shanxi, Hunan, Sichuan, Ningxia and other jurisdictions properly handled cases of rural land transfer, forest rights transfer and shareholding cooperation, to safeguard the legitimate rights and interests of rural business entities and to help revitalize industries in underdeveloped areas. People's courts in Guizhou and Tibet, as well as in Nujiang, and Linxia actively served poverty-relief relocation work, safeguarded farmers' right of land contractual management and the right to use homesteads, resolved disputes over the production and marketing of agricultural products, and promoted rural economic and social development.

Helped protect our blue skies, clear waters, and clean lands. People's courts at various levels concluded 268 thousand environmental resource cases of first instance. We also concluded 1,953 environmental public interest litigation cases filed by procuratorial organs and social organizations, and held the legal responsibility of those who destroyed the Sanqing Mountain Jumang Peak and its ecological environment. People's courts in Anhui heard the case of illegal discharge of toxic substances to Yangtze River through concealed pipes and polluting the environment, so that the offenders not only bore criminal liability, but also fulfilled the obligations of ecological environment restoration. The newly-set environmental resource courts in Nanjing of Jiangsu Province and Lanzhou of Gansu Province could make centralized management of environmental resource cases in the corresponding jurisdictions, putting into practice the principles of ecological priority and green development. People's courts along the Yangtze River and the Yellow River strengthened judicial cooperation and promoted ecological protection and systematic governance of large rivers.

Provided judicial assistance to the supply-side structural reform. In conjunction with the National Development and Reform Commission, we issued a reform plan for accelerating the withdrawal of market participants, reducing the cost of withdrawal, promoting the flow of production factors and the transformation and upgrading of enterprises. We gave full play to the important role of the bankruptcy system to promote the survival of the fittest in the market, to resolve local financial risks, and maintain social harmony and stability. We properly concluded 4,626 bankruptcy and reorganization cases, involving 678.8 billion yuan claims, which advanced the smooth and orderly clearing of "zombie enterprises", helped 482 promising companies walk out of predicament through reorganization and saved 108 thousand employees of their jobs. The people's courts in Tianjin provided judicial support to the reorganization and reform of state-owned enterprises in accordance with the law and promoted the resolution of debt risks of state-owned enterprises. Tonghua People's Court, through the bankruptcy and reorganization procedures, helped the Tonggang Group successfully achieve the "debt-to-equity swap", resolved the huge debt crisis and protected the interests of creditors and employees. People's courts in Huaibei explored the settlement mode of real estate enterprises bankruptcy to promote healthy development of real estate market.

Provided judicial assistance to the implementation of the regional coordinated development strategy. The SPC issued special opinions to serve the planning construction and innovative development of the Xiong'an New District. People's courts in Beijing, Tianjin, and Hebei properly resolved disputes over major projects to serve the coordinated development of Beijing-Tianjin-Hebei region and the preparation for the Winter Olympics and Winter Paralympics. People's courts in Shanghai, Jiangsu, Zhejiang, and Anhui improved their judicial coordinating level for the better integrated growth within the Yangtze River

Delta region. People's courts in Liaoning, Jilin and Heilongjiang delivered judicial services to focus on improving business environment to revitalize the Northeast Rustbelt in an all-round way. People's courts in Guangdong focused on building a more just and effective judicial environment, in an aim to better serve the development of the Guangdong-Hong Kong-Macao Greater Bay Area and the Shenzhen Pilot Demonstration Zone.

Provided judicial assistance to the development of digital economy. We strengthened the judicial protection of data rights, which was conducive to the use of big data, the development of digital economy and the protection of people's personal privacy. Judicature should create a competitive, open and inclusive environment for digital economy. People's courts at various levels properly handled cases involving new transactions, new models and new formats in accordance with the law, to ensure the healthy development of digital economy, promote deep integration of digital and real economy, and provide new momentum for high-quality economic development. We heard new cases of artificial intelligence and online game copyrights, to strengthen the protection of digital copyright and digital content products. We enhanced protection of data security and personal privacy, severely punished the crime of infringing on personal information, and tried cases such as unauthorized reading of users' address book information on the mobile phone application and misuse of personal credit data on the online credit platform; we accurately applied the "Notification of Deletion" rule, and ordered online platforms that distributed defamatory comments to delete them at the request of the victim.

Provided judicial assistance to higher-standard opening up. People's Courts at various levels concluded 17 thousand foreign-related civil and commercial cases of first instance, and 16 thousand maritime and maritime trade cases of first instance. We formulated judicial interpretations of the Foreign Investment Law to equally protect the legitimate rights and interests of Chinese and foreign investors according to law. We issued opinions on the construction of the "Belt and Road Initiative" and on the construction of the Lingang New Area of the Shanghai Pilot Free Trade Zone. People's courts in Tianjin, Hubei, Guangxi, Chongqing, Sichuan and other jurisdictions actively improved the judicial guarantee measures in the Pilot Free Trade Zone. The people's courts in Hainan opened a free trade port judicial service platform to provide judicial credit reporting services for Chinese and foreign investors free of charge. The Nanjing Maritime Court, based on its geographical advantages, actively served the development of marine economy. The Qingdao Maritime Court properly resolved the distrain of M/V Nerissa and avoided huge losses for all parties involved. The foreign party specifically renamed the ship "Respect" to pay tribute to the rule of law in China.

III. Adhering to the principles of administrating justice for the people and maintaining judicial fairness to better serve social justice

Promoted the core socialist values. We held high the banner of patriotism, severely punished the crime of insulting the national flag, the national emblem and the national anthem, and declared the state to be solemn and inviolable. We concluded 22 heroic protection public interest litigation cases and seriously investigated legal responsibility for infringement of the rights and interests of Fang Zhimin, Dong Cunrui, Huang Jiguang, and the firefighting warriors sacrificed in the Muli County fire, to defend their glory. We carried out the "Implementation Outline for Citizens' Moral Construction in the New Era", integrated core socialist values into judicial work, and guided people to be kinder by rule of law. The SPC and the National Development and Reform Commission improved the joint discipline mechanism against people who defaulted on court orders, encouraged honesty and trustworthiness, and punished dishonesty and breaches of contract. We tried cases of online crowdfunding refunds, to standardize online public welfare behavior and to protect the traditional virtues of helping the needy and being credible and honest.

Maintain social justice. People's courts at various levels concluded 9.393 million civil cases of first instance, including 1.44 million people's livelihood-related cases involving education, employment, medical care, housing, consumption and social security. We severely punished crimes against persons with disabilities and facilitated disabled people's lawsuits, in order to protect their lawful rights and interests. We actively participated in the "wage protection" action, strengthened the trial enforcement of cases of wage arrears of migrant workers, increased the punishment of the crime of refusing to pay labor remuneration, and helped migrant workers to recover wages of 10.66 billion yuan. We distributed a total of 1.12 billion yuan judicial assistance subsidy to help people involved in prosecution to get rid of their difficulties. The SPC and the Ministry of Human Resources and Social Security issued regulatory documents to promote women's equal employment, and created a fairer environment of employment. We properly tried cases involving pregnant female workers' being dismissed and graduates subjected to regional discrimination in job hunting, and pushed forward a unified pilot for compensation standards for personal injury of urban and rural residents, to ensure fair rights, opportunities and rules in accordance with the law.

Promoted the construction of a harmonious family. We deepened the reform on family matters adjudication. The SPC worked with the All China Women's Federation to improve the protection mechanism for women's and children's rights, and paid more attention to the protection of family members' dignity, safety and emotions. We concluded 1.85 million marriage and family cases, intensified the anti-domestic violence policy, and issued 2,004 personal safety protection orders in time. People's courts in Xinxiang of Henan Province, Xiaogan of Hubei Province and Yulin of Guangxi Province improved the mediation of marriage and family disputes, and tried to reintegrate the couples whose relationship had not truly broken down, so that children can enjoy the warmth of family integrity; we let couples whose relationship had broken down divorce to avoid a family tragedy. We severely punished the crimes of abuse, abandonment and injury to the elderly; we concluded 26 thousand cases of elderly maintenance to safeguard the legitimate rights and interests of the elderly; the family courts smartly resolved household chores, properly resolved the disputes of maintenance and upbringing, educating Chinese people to respect the elders, love the children and pass on our virtues from generation to generation, and let family-centered tradition exist forever.

Protected the healthy growth of the minor. We improved the juvenile justice system and adhered to the round-table trial. Judge Chen Haiyi of the Guangzhou Intermediate People's Court used mother-like care to help the juvenile offenders walk into a new life. By organizing and observing the juvenile court, we let the juvenile experience justice and learn legal knowledge. We severely punished crimes against children's physical and mental health according to law, and sentenced to death a group of criminals like Zhao Zhiyong and He Long with extremely serious crimes who sexually abused children.

The SPC and the Ministry of Civil Affairs issued opinions to strengthen the protection of factually unattended children. People's courts in Guizhou and other jurisdictions specially formulated documents to protect the legal rights and interests of left-behind children in rural areas, so that every child would be bathed in the sun of the rule of law. We strengthened the prevention and treatment of bullying on campus and concluded 4,192 relevant cases. The SPC and the Ministry of Education improved the mechanism for handling campus safety incidents and punished crimes of "school troubles" pursuant to law. We actively promoted the joint pilot mechanism of judicial protection and administration, family, school and community protection, and used the rule of law to protect children's healthy growth.

Safeguarded the interests of national defense and the legitimate rights and interests of military personnel and their families. We fully completed the task of the cessation of military paid services, during which five courts were awarded "advanced agencies" and 15 people were awarded "advanced individuals" jointly by the Ministry of Human Resources and Social Security, the Political Work Department and the Logistics Support Department of China's Central Military Commission. We researched and promulgated 15 measures to organize special forces, open green channels, and provide judicial services for the next phase regarding the cessation of military paid services. We severely punished crimes like sabotage of military facilities, fraud involving impersonation of soldiers, and concluded 484 relevant cases. The military courts steadily pushed forward military administrative pilot trials and safeguarded the lawful rights and interests of army officers and soldiers according to law. People's courts in Hunan, Chongqing, Sichuan and other jurisdictions improved the cooperation mechanism among military and local courts. People's courts in Linyi of Shandong Province and Xinyang of Henan Province carried forward the good traditions and good experiences of the old revolutionary bases, and conscientiously did their job in protecting the military-related rights. These measures greatly promoted the solidarity between the civilians and military personnel.

Protected the legitimate rights and interests of Hong Kong, Macao and Taiwan compatriots, overseas Chinese, as well as returned overseas Chinese and their families. People's courts at various levels concluded 27 thousand cases related to Hong Kong, Macau and Taiwan, executed 9,648 requests of judicial assistance related to Hong Kong, Macao and Taiwan counterparts, and concluded 2,475 cases involving overseas Chinese. The coverage of almost all areas of civil and commercial judicial assistance between the Mainland and Hong Kong was realized. We established a network platform for judicial assistance between the Mainland and Macau. We issued 36 judicial measures beneficial to Taiwan to protect the legitimate rights and interests of Taiwan compatriots and Taiwan enterprises on an equal basis. We also actively created internship conditions for law students in

Hong Kong, Macao and Taiwan to enhance their understanding of the judicial system of their motherland.

Guided members of society to enhance public awareness and rule awareness. In modern society, people's work and life are inseparable from public space. The normative public behavior is the foundation of social vitality, harmony and order. When handling the cases happening in public spaces, people's courts took into account the law, common sense and humanity, distinguished right from wrong, punished evil and encouraged good, and strived to achieve the unification of legal and social effects. In the case of "sudden death when being obstructed for hitting a child and running", the court decided that the obstructer had no responsibility, which was an encouragement to righteousness and bravery. In the case of "the patient injuring himself while assaulting a doctor", the court revised the judgement and decided that the doctor was in justifiable defense, resolutely saying no to "blurring the line between right and wrong". In the first case of "WeChat group leader kicking out members", the people's court supported proper management within the WeChat group, preventing the online community from becoming an extrajudicial place. In the case of "climbing a tree to pick waxberries but falling off to death", the court decided that the village committee had not violated the safety guarantee obligation, so that the law-abiding people did not have to be accountable for others' faults. In the case of "drowning when walking dog on ice", the court decided that people who assumed the risk bore their own responsibilities. In the case of "drowning of the thief when escaping and jumping into the river", the court ruled that those who chased the thief were not accountable, and demonstrated that those who behaved righteously did not bear excessive duty of care. Through a series of case trials, we resolved the legal and moral hazards that had long plagued the masses, such as "helping or not", "persuading or not", "chasing or not", "saving or not", "doing or not" and "taking or not". We resolutely prevented the "line blurring" approach, like "whoever disturbing, outrageous or injured can finally get what he/she wants". We should make justice powerful, reasonable and humane; let the masses embrace warmth, observance and security, and become good citizens under the rule of law.

IV. We built a convenient and efficient mechanism for resolving conflicts and disputes, and actively participated in social governance

Resolving conflicts and disputes is an important part of social governance. The people's court is the adjudication organ that resolves conflicts and disputes and solves people's claims. Resolving disputes fairly and efficiently is an important responsibility of the people's courts to participate in social governance, and is also an important part to promote the modernization of the national governance system and governance capabilities.

Unblocked channels for dispute resolution. We consolidated the achievement of the reform of case filing and registration mechanism. We promoted case filing on the spot, self-filing and online filing, and resolutely prevented the difficulty of case filing from rebounding. The court opened its doors, but not played solo. We must adhere to and develop the "Fengqiao experience" in the new era, integrate it into the social governance system led by the Party committee, rely on people and social organizations to effectively prevent and resolve disputes. People's courts at various levels put the non-litigation dispute resolution methods in the forefront, improved the comprehensive use of people's mediation, administrative mediation and judicial mediation, and connected non-litigation and litigation, and gave full play to the function of the people's court mediation platform to resolve disputes online, so that internal conflicts among people could be dissolved faster and more effectively. The courts in Yunnan, Qinghai, Ningxia, Xinjiang and the Production and Construction Corps innovated mediation mechanisms with ethnic characteristics to safeguard the legitimate rights and interests of people of all ethnic groups and promote national unity. The courts in Zhejiang summarized and promoted the practices of Putuo and Anji, actively participated in the overall pattern of social governance, and effectively resolved the contradiction at the beginning and at the grassroots.

Established a one-stop mechanism of multiple dispute resolution and litigation service. We promoted the separation of cases into simple cases and complicated ones, trivial cases and major ones, and summary trial cases and standard ones, so as to establish a one-stop dispute resolution mechanism of mediation, speedy decision, and fast trial in the litigation service center to speed up the realization of fairness and justice. The litigation service centers of all the courts nationwide resolved 8.497 million cases, of which the average trial time of fast-track cases was 49.2% shorter than that of first-instance civil and commercial cases. We unblocked access to litigation service channels, never let the masses have nowhere to plea retrial, and never ignore their demands. Litigation service centers could provide one-stop, one-network, and one-number litigation services. People's courts in Jiangxi, Hunan and other jurisdictions set up self-service litigation facilities in rural communities to make it more convenient for people to participate in litigation.

Promoted cross-jurisdiction litigation services. We carried out cross-jurisdiction litigation services nationwide. Parties could choose the nearest court to submit a case filing application and avoid traveling. The Beijing-Tianjin-Hebei, Yangtze River Delta and Pearl River Delta regions took the lead in realizing cross-jurisdiction case filing. The national intermediate, primary courts and maritime courts achieved full coverage of cross-jurisdiction case filing services. The new model of "pleading in the community" effectively solved the problem of inconvenience for people in remote jurisdictions.

Resolved disputes based on urban and rural grassroots units. We took the advantage of 10,759 people's tribunals across the country, actively participated in county-level grassroots governance, and mediated and concluded a total of 4.731 million cases. People's tribunals in Yan'an, Xunwu and Liangdang let people tell their own stories directly and the judge explain laws to resolve conflicts and disputes in a timely manner and serve the revitalization of the countryside. The "Horseback courtroom" and the "back basket judge" trekked into the fields and people's homes, and endeavored to follow up wherever there was judicial demand.

V. We consolidated the achievement of "basically solving the difficulties in enforcement" to ensure high quality accomplishment of the enforcement work.

After achieving the goal of "basically solving the difficulties in enforcement" as scheduled, the people's courts at various levels determined not to relax and continued to consolidate the good results, strode towards the goal of solving enforcement difficulties. In 2019, people's courts nationwide accepted 10.414 million enforcement cases and concluded 9.547 million cases, with an enforcement amount of 1.7 trillion yuan, up by 17.4%, 22.4%, and 10.8% year-on-year respectively. Various enforcement indicators saw improvement and stability, and China's special enforcement system, mechanism and model became complete.

Deepened comprehensive governance and source governance. We conscientiously implemented the "2019 No. 1 Document" of the Rule of Law Commission of the CPC Central Committee, improved the cross-departmental system supervision and joint disciplinary mechanism, and consolidated the pattern of comprehensive governance and enforcement. The Provincial Rule of Law Commission of Hebei, Jiangxi, Henan, Shaanxi and other provinces comprehensively formulated and implemented opinions on the rule of law. The Standing Committee of the Hunan Provincial People's Congress issued a document specifically to support the people's courts to solve the enforcement difficulty. We conscientiously adopted the deliberation opinions of the deputies, formulated and implemented the five-year development outline of the enforcement work, improved the long-term mechanism, and made sure that the standards and the intensity would not be reduced after the hard work. We formulated opinions on lawyers' participation in enforcement and fully utilized the professional strength. In accordance with the deployment of the NPC Standing Committee, we provided our support to the legislation of the Civil Mandatory Enforcement Law, to improve a better law enforcement system with Chinese characteristics.

Enhanced enforcement with goodwill and in a civilized manner. We adhered to strict and fair enforcement according to law, resolutely cracked down on evasion and resistance to enforcement, and protected the legitimate rights and interests of the successful parties. We drew up enforcement opinions that emphasized goodwill and civilized manners, optimized measures such as seizure and evaluation, and minimized the impact on the production and operation of enterprises. For companies whose capital chain was temporarily broken but still had potential for survival after saving, we guided them to adopt the methods of settlement and phased implementation, mergers and reorganization to fulfill enforcement. We established mechanisms such as graded management of credit punishment and restoration of dishonesty, made sure the procedures for punishment of dishonesty were strictly followed, and that credit punishment was precisely executed. We timely removed 2.083 million person-times of dishonest list according to law, up by 19.3% year-on-year. We changed the enforcement working philosophy from the previous punishment-oriented to equal emphasis on punishment and incentives. People's courts in Ningbo of Zhejiang Province and Ningde of Fujian Province introduced a positive incentive mechanism for spontaneous performance, which greatly increased the spontaneous performance rate and created a social atmosphere of trustworthiness.

Strengthened efforts to solve the people's pressing concerns. For cases involving people's livelihood, finance, and arrears in accounts of private enterprises, we concentratedly carried out the special enforcement actions. During the centralized enforcement period, people's courts across the country concluded 210 thousand cases involving people's livelihood, and the amount of enforcement was 9.8 billion yuan, which made people feel more fulfilled. We concluded 470 thousand financial cases of enforcement, and the amount reached 200 billion yuan. We concluded the enforcement of 5,870 cases of arrears in private enterprises, and the total amount was 12.7 billion yuan, which protected the legitimate rights and interests of private enterprises and small and medium-sized enterprises (SMEs).

VI. We deepened the reform of the judiciary system and accelerated the building of smart courts, to improve judicial quality, efficiency and credibility

Justice and efficiency are the eternal value pursued by people's courts. Facing the continuous rapid growth of cases worldwide, especially civil and commercial cases, Chinese courts must work out our own solutions. We can neither take the path of continuous expansion of staff, nor can we restrict filing, select filing or reject people's appeals. We must rely on deepening judicial reform and building a smart court, to accelerate the modernization of the judicial system and capacity.

Introduced a more in-depth and comprehensive reform of the judicial system. We implemented the opinions on the comprehensively deepening reforms in the political and legal fields, and promulgated the fifth five-year reform outline of people's courts, to promote the integration, synergy and efficiency of various reform systems. We implemented the newly-revised Organization Law of the People's Courts and Judges' Law, improved the supporting mechanism, and promoted the transformation of the advantages of the socialist judicial system with Chinese characteristics into governance effectiveness. We implemented the People's Assessors Law and expanded the scope of participation, with 3.407 million cases of assessors participating in the trial nationwide. According to the authorization of the NPC Standing Committee, we carried out the pilot program of the reform of separation of cases into simple cases and complicated ones under civil procedures in 20 cities of 15 provinces, to stimulate judicial effectiveness through systematic innovation and to meet the more diverse, efficient and convenient dispute resolution demand of our people.

Fully implemented the judicial accountability system. We improved the trial power operation system of orderly delegation of power, scientific allocation of power, standardized use of power, and strict restrictions on power, formulated a list of trial powers and responsibilities, clarified the powers and responsibilities of the court presidents and chief judges of divisions, trial organization and judges, and specified the court presidents' and chief judges' of divisions trial supervision and management responsibilities, so that power must exist with accountability, use of power must bear its accountability, negligence must be held accountable, and abuse of power must be held accountable. We gave full play to the role of judicial interpretation and guiding cases, promoted a mandatory search mechanism for cases of similarity and of relevance, improved the working mechanism of the adjudication committee, and promoted the unification of decision standards. We deepened the judges' post system reform, promoted the selection of judges, improved the provincial level coordination, dynamic adjustment and exchange & exit mechanism for the number of judges, so that there were outs and ins and the fittest may survive. Shanxi, Inner Mongolia and Chongqing meticulously implemented the policy of duty performance, to inspire judges to handle cases impartially.

Explored a new Internet judicial model. We fully utilized the leading role of the Internet courts in Beijing, Hangzhou and Guangzhou, in order to promote the "online trial of online cases", improve the rules of online litigation, and let the public enjoy the convenience of online litigation. We fully promoted the "China Mobile Micro-Court", led the development of electronic litigation services to the mobile terminal, and took the lead in the development trend of mobile electronic litigation in the world. We heard "live streaming selling" cases to clarify cyberspace behavior norms, rights boundaries and responsibilities. We heard illegal "shadow traffic" cases to promote the rule of law in cyberspace governance. We held the World Internet Forum on the Rule of

Law in Wuzhen, to deepen international cooperation in Internet justice and establish a cyberspace community of shared future.

Promoted in-depth application of technologies of big data and blockchain. We deepened the application of judicial big data and completed 806 special reports to provide a reference for the adjudication of objects falling from high, the protection of the rights of women and children etc. We established a national unified judicial blockchain platform, innovated online evidence recording methods, and promoted to solve the problems of difficulty in obtaining, recording and certifying e-evidence. The application of blockchain smart contract technology in enforcement would improve the standardization of enforcement. We promoted applications such as speech recognition in court hearings, intelligent error correction of documents, and intelligent push of "Faxin" to provide smart assistance for judges in handling cases and for people in litigation.

Deepened the sunshine justice. As of April this year, the website of China Judgments Online published 91.95 million documents; the website of China Judicial Process Information Online disclosed 29 million cases and 1.5 billion pieces of information to the parties, making fairness and justice stand in the sun. The website of China Trial Hearing Online published 6.96 million cases in live streaming with 23.7 billion person-times watching in total. The online hearing of courts has become a new platform for the masses to respect law and abide by the law. After years of practice, the open, transparent, dynamic and convenient judicial mechanism in the sun has become more mature, and has enriched the development of socialist legal civilization.

The judicial reform and the smart court, as the "two wheels of a car and two wings of a bird", have modernized the trial system and improved the trial capacity of people's courts; they have effectively improved the quality and efficiency of trials. In 2019, judges of people's courts at various levels handled 228 cases per capita, an increase of 13.4% year-on-year; the rate of litigation conclusion after the first trial was 89.2%, and 98.2% after the second trial; the total number of complaint letters and visits, and the number of complaints and visits to Beijing decreased by 13.3% and 40% respectively year-on-year; the average trial period of Internet court cases was 42 days, which was 57.1% shorter than the traditional model.

VII. We adhered to the directions of revolution, normalization, specialization and professionalism, and improved the quality construction of the working team of the people's courts

Always put the Party's political building high on our agenda. We studied and implemented the Xi Jinping Thought on Socialism with Chinese Characteristics for a New Era, used it to arm the mind, guide practice and promote work, and firmly adhered to the Party's absolute leadership over judicial work. We carried out the thematic education campaign of "staying true to the Party's founding mission", accepted the profound ideological and political education, and guided the broad court officers to remember their mission and faithfully perform their duties. We conscientiously implemented the "Regulations on the Political and Legal Work of the Communist Party of China" and put into practice the party's leadership in all aspects and in the whole process of our work. We continued to focus on party building and team building to improve our trial, and strived to create a model organ that reassured the Party Central Committee and satisfied the people. We seriously accepted the inspection by the Party Central Committee and paid close attention to the rectification of problems. We carried out in-depth learning activities of Zou Bihua. A number of advanced models like Li Qingjun of the new era of justice for the people and fairness emerged from people's courts across the country. 532 groups and 661 individuals were commended by the relevant central authorities. Song Yushui from a court in Beijing, Tan Yan from a court in Liaoning, Sun Bo from a court in Heilongjiang, Zou Bihua from a court in Shanghai and Huang Zhili from a court in Fujian were awarded the "Most Beautiful Struggler". They interpreted the original true goal of the people's judge with loyalty and even their life.

Continued to strengthen judicial capacity building. We provided professional trainings to 615 thousand court officers. We innovated the training mechanism of legal talents, deepened cooperation with colleges and universities, actively participated in the special lectures of China's political and legal practice, so as to promote the close integration of judicial practice and teaching and research. We selected 851 judges to participate in foreign-related training and exchanges, and cultivated professional foreign-related judicial talents. We strengthened grassroots infrastructure construction, improved grassroots working conditions, and increased support for the construction of courts and personnel training in the old revolutionary base areas, ethnic areas, border areas, and poverty-stricken areas. We trained 1,345 bilingual judges, and people's courts in Inner Mongolia, Tibet, Qinghai and Xinjiang actively participated in the "Bilingual Legal Culture Publishing Project" to better meet the judicial needs of people in ethnic areas.

Worked ceaselessly to improve party conduct and enforce party discipline. We strictly implemented the CPC Central Committee's eight-point decision and its implementation rules. We solved the problems of formalism and bureaucracy that plagued the grassroots. Combining thematic education campaign, we deepened and focused on the central rectification of prominent problems and effectively solved the problem of "black in the light". We strictly implemented the "two responsibilities for one post", so that negligence must be treated. We made supervision inwardly, and severely punished judicial corruption with a zero-tolerance attitude, and resolutely eliminated the black sheep.

The SPC investigated and punished 11 officers who violated disciplines and laws. People's courts at various levels investigated and punished 1,374 officers who violated disciplines and laws by abusing the power of trial and enforcement, of which 115 were accounted for criminal responsibilities. We made in-depth self-examination and self-correction, comprehensive and complete rectification of outstanding issues that affected judicial integrity, such as cases of illegal interference, violations of avoidance, acting as brokers in litigation, and anonymous agency by relatives and friends. We carried out in-depth warning education, used cases of violations of law and discipline as negative teaching materials, drew profound lessons, drew inferences from others, repaired loopholes, improved mechanisms, and created a clean and upright judicial environment.

VIII. We took the initiative to accept supervision and improve and correct the work of people's courts

We accepted the supervision of the NPC in accordance with the law, earnestly implemented the resolutions of the Second Session of the 13th NPC and the opinions and suggestions put forward by the deputies, refined the division of labor item by item, and strengthened the follow-up work after supervision. We conscientiously implemented the deliberations of the NPC Standing Committee's special report on the difficulty of enforcement, and we made a report specifically on the implementation progress. We made a report to the NPC Standing Committee on the criminal trial work in order to promote the development of criminal trial in the new era based on the review opinions. We handled 355 deputy suggestions seriously and 395 daily suggestions. We communicated closely throughout the process and accepted the deputies' opinions. Deputies of the NPC were invited to inspect the courts, participate in conferences, and attend court hearings and other activities in 1,492 person-times; we specially invited deputies to jointly carry out investigations on judicial protection of the ecological environment in the Yangtze River and the Yellow River basins. We seriously accepted democratic supervision, handled 173 proposals from the CPPCC, visited and received 180 members of the CPPCC; we strengthened communication with democratic parties, the Federation of Industry and Commerce and non-party personages, and listened to their opinions widely. We deepened the implementation of the Supervision Law and voluntarily accepted supervision to court staff from the supervisory authority. We accepted litigation supervision by procuratorial organs in accordance with the law, dealt with protest cases impartially, and carefully handled procuratorial suggestions. We widely accept social supervision, and actively carried out research activities involving special supervisors, specially invited consultants, experts and scholars, as well as inviting them to attend the adjudicative committee. We increased interaction with the news media, carried out all media live broadcast activities, and proactively accepted public opinion supervision.

Fellow deputies, the development and progress of the people's courts' work over the past year were fundamentally attributed to the strong leadership of the CPC Central Committee with Comrade Xi Jinping at its core, and to the scientific guidance of Xi Jinping Thought on Socialism with Chinese Characteristics for a New Era. We owe our achievements to the diligent supervision of the NPC and its Standing Committee, the strong support of the State Council, democratic supervision from the CPPCC, supervision from the National Supervisory Commission and the Supreme People's Procuratorate, democratic supervision of democratic parties, Federation of Industry and Commerce, people's organizations and non-party personages, care, support and assistance of local Party committees and governments at all levels, NPC delegates, CPPCC members and people from all walks of life. On this occasion, I would like to extend, on behalf of the SPC, our heartfelt gratitude!

We are also keenly aware that there are still many problems and difficulties ahead. **First,** discrepancy is still observed between what our judges can offer and what we are expected to deliver in the new era in terms of judicial concepts and judicial capabilities. We should also improve our capability in responding to risks and challenges and providing services for high-quality development. **Second,** the research on the new situation and new problems brought by the economic and social development to the judiciary is insufficient, and there is a problem that the standard of judgement in some cases is not uniform. **Third,** the comprehensive supporting reform of the judicial system has not been implemented, and the trial management system and the supervision and control mechanism for the operation of trial power are not sound enough. **Fourth,** there is a shortage of high-quality professional trial talents in the fields of IPR, Internet, and foreign affairs, and the talent training mechanism needs to be improved. **Fifth,** the issues of wrong judicial working styles and corruption occur from time to time. Some officers use cases for personal gain, make power and money transactions, and even act as a "protective umbrella" for the evil forces. **Sixth,** some courts have a dilemma between the number of judges and the number of cases, and the pressure of handling cases is high. Some primary courts in remote areas have serious problems in recruiting and retaining people. We will take effective measures to solve the above problems under the leadership of the Party.

Work Arrangements in the Next Phase

The year of 2020 is the last year of building a well-off society in an all-round way and accomplishing the 13th Five-Year Plan. It is also the critical year for a complete victory over the battle against poverty. The COVID-19 epidemic has brought unprecedented impact on China's economic and social development, as well as on the international and domestic situation. The challenges facing China's development are unprecedented, and the challenges facing judicial work are unprecedented. The task is very arduous. The people's courts must adhere to the guidance of Xi Jinping Thought on Socialism with Chinese Characteristics for a New Era, strengthen our consciousness of the need to maintain political integrity, think in big-picture terms, follow the leadership core, and keep in alignment with the central Party leadership; stay confident in the path, theory, system, and culture of socialism with Chinese characteristics; and uphold General Secretary Xi Jinping's core position on the Party Central Committee and in the Party as a whole, and uphold the Party Central Committee's authority and its centralized, unified leadership; fully implement the guiding principles of the Party's 19th National Congress and the second, third, and fourth plenary sessions of its 19th Central Committee and the Central Political and Legal Work Conference. We will thoroughly study and follow the important speeches when General Secretary Xi Jinping chaired the Politburo Standing Committee meeting and listened to the work report of the SPC Party Group. We will earnestly implement the resolution of this session, bear in mind the strategic overall situation of the great rejuvenation of the Chinese nation and the major changes in the world in a century. We will continue with the Party's absolute leadership in judicial work, take a people-centered approach, adhere to the general tone of progress in stability, be good at turning crises into opportunities, fully perform responsibilities, and maintain the overall situation of economic development and social stability in accordance with the law. We will deliver strong judicial services and support for coordinating the promotion of epidemic prevention and control and economic and social development, ensuring the completion of the decisive battle against poverty and completely building a well-off society in an all-round way.

First, provide services to guarantee regular epidemic prevention and control and comprehensive restoration of economic and social order. We will make a good judicial response in the regular epidemic prevention and control, protect people's lives and health according to law, give full play to the role of justice in promoting development, stabilizing expectations, and protecting people's livelihood, and ensure the effective implementation of the national policy of benefiting enterprises according to law. We will deliver accurate services to ensure stability on the six fronts and security in the six areas. We will continue to bring the non-litigation dispute resolution mechanism to the forefront, and focus on the use of mediation, settlement enforcements and other means to properly resolve conflicts and disputes caused by the epidemic, so as to guarantee regular epidemic prevention and control through rule of law. We will accurately apply force majeure rules according to law, reasonably balance the interests of the parties, and guide all parties to share risks and overcome difficulties. We will adhere to the concept of goodwill and civilized enforcement, resolutely put an end to the excessive and chaotic sealing, effectively use the aforementioned flexible measures, and try our best to maintain the operating value of corporate property. Through bankruptcy, reorganization, reconciliation and other procedures, we will help enterprises resolve crises and overcome troubles. We will make full use of judicial means and do our utmost to ensure the survival of enterprises, especially SMEs, and to protect and promote employment. We will properly resolve disputes in areas such as investment and consumption, new-type infrastructure, etc., and create a favorable environment for the rule of law for the implementation of the strategy of expanding domestic demand. We will crack down malicious debt evasion and debt discarding behaviors. We will hear all kinds of foreign-related cases in accordance with the law fairly and efficiently, serve the expansion of opening up to the outside world and the "Belt and Road" high-quality development, and support the construction of Hainan Free Trade Port. We will deepen international judicial exchanges and cooperation, promote global anti-epidemic legal cooperation, and serve to build a community with a shared future for mankind. Chinese people's courts will strictly abide by international law and generally accept basic principles of international relations, and resolutely defend China's judicial sovereignty and national security.

Second, focus on serving to build a safe China at a higher level. We will severely crack down on the penetration, destruction, subversion, and separatist activities of the hostile forces. We will punish, according to law, various crimes that affect the regular epidemic prevention and control. We will resolutely maintain national security, biological security, ecological security, public health security and social stability. We will promote and improve the public health system based on judicial functions, and strengthen and improve the public health legal guarantee. We will punish duty crimes in accordance with the law, and promote integrated services where people do not dare to corrupt, cannot corrupt, and do not want to corrupt. We will strictly punish crimes in public safety and people's livelihood, and strengthen research and response to new crimes. We will enhance judicial protection of human rights and protect lawyers' right to practice in accordance with the law. We will deepen the special fight against organized gang-related crimes and try relevant cases in a fair and efficient manner, so that each case can withstand the test of law and history, and let the people obtain a greater sense of security.

Third, focus on serving high-quality economic development. We will improve judicial policies holding close to the decisive battle against poverty and building a moderately well-off society in an all-around way. We will severely punish all kinds of crimes related to agriculture, rural areas and farmers, deepen poverty alleviation with rule of law, strengthen judicial guarantees for consumer poverty alleviation, employment poverty alleviation and industrial poverty alleviation, improve financial and environmental resource trial, and provide effective judicial services for the three tough battles. By generalizing experiences of people's courts in Beijing, Shanghai and other jurisdictions, we will actively create a more stable, fair, transparent, and predictable legal business environment. We will strengthen judicial protection of property rights and IPR, and protect business secrets. We will strengthen the protection of data rights and personal information, and severely punish crimes such as revealing and selling citizens' personal information, in order to serve the healthy development of the digital economy. We will improve the judicial service policy measures and our service quality for the coordinated development of Beijing-Tianjin-Hebei region, the construction of the Guangdong-Hong Kong-Macao Greater Bay Area, the development of the Yangtze River Economic Belt, the integrated development of the Yangtze River Delta, the ecological protection and high-quality development of the Yellow River Basin, the large-scale development of western China, the comprehensive revitalization of the Northeast, the rise of central China and the construction of Chengdu-Chongqing double cities economic circle.

Fourth, strengthen judicial protection for people's livelihood. We will earnestly implement the Civil Code after deliberation and approval, comprehensively clean up civil judicial interpretations, formulate new supporting judicial interpretations, enhance learning and training, improve civil adjudication capability and standard, protect the legal rights and interests of civil subjects according to law, adjust civil relations, and maintain social and economic order. We will continue to integrate the requirements of socialist core values into judicial trials, fulfill the requirement of "whoever enforces the law shall popularize the law", and promote uprightness. The enforcement work is always on the road. We will improve the long-term mechanism for effectively solving the difficulties of enforcement, and make it fair, standardized and civilized. We will actively participate in municipal social governance, give play to the role of people's tribunals, and serve the construction of rural areas under the rule of law. We will safeguard national defense interests according to law by protecting military personnel, their families and veterans' lawful rights and interests. We will adhere to the people's voice as the first signal, and continue to solve the problems that people are concerned about. We will enhance the judicial protection of women, children, the elderly and the disabled. We will resolutely correct regional, gender and other discrimination in employment according to law, resolutely correct the act of illegal termination of the labor contract relationship of patients with COVID-19 in accordance with law, address the problem of unpaid wages for migrant workers in accordance with the law, and safeguard the right of workers to fair employment.

Fifth, advance the modernization of the trial system and trial capacity. We will conscientiously implement the opinions of the people's court on the Fourth Plenary Session of the 19th Central Committee of the CPC, and improve the effectiveness of the judicial promotion of governance system and modernization of governance capabilities. We will review the reform, consolidate the reform achievements, implement the opinions on deepening comprehensive and integrated reforms over the judicial responsibility system, enhance guidance to lower level courts, and improve the reform effectiveness. We will deepen the reform of categorizing and distributing civil procedure based on complexity. We will improve administrative litigation court hearing procedure and comprehensively improve the effectiveness of one-stop diversified dispute resolution and litigation services. We will study new situations, solve new problems, and promote the unification of verdict standards. We will deepen judicial openness. We will consolidate and expand the achievements of smart court construction and application during the epidemic period, improve the Internet judicial model.

Sixth, build a team of loyal, clean and competent court staff. We will strengthen the political construction of the Party in the people's courts, consolidate and deepen the achievements in the thematic education campaign, enhance talent training and team management, and forge a high-quality team with excellent politics, professionalism, responsibility, discipline and working style. We will enhance infrastructure construction at the grassroots level and support the development of courts in old revolutionary base areas, ethnic areas, border areas and poverty-stricken areas. We will seriously make rectification after inspection. We will consciously accept the supervision of the NPC, democratic supervision and supervision in all aspects. We will consolidate the main responsibility for comprehensive and strict governance of the Party, resolutely eliminate formalism and bureaucracy, strictly enforce the "three regulations" and other iron bans that prevent external and internal personnel from interfering with the judiciary, so that there is no room for black box operations, and judicial corruption cannot be hidden below. We will carry out warning education of "explaining morality by case, explaining discipline by case, and interpreting law by case", and severely punish judicial corruption with a zero-tolerance attitude. We will persist in the main theme of "strict" for a long time, and ensure fair justice with clean justice. We will carry forward the spirit of struggle, enhance fighting skills, resolve conflicts and disputes with judicial responsibility, and achieve fairness and equity with justice.

Fellow deputies, the people's courts take great responsibilities and sacred missions in 2020. We will, under the strong leadership of the CPC central committee with Comrade Xi Jinping at its core, follow the Xi Jinping Thought on Socialism with Chinese Characteristics for a New Era, faithfully perform the duties entrusted by the Constitution and laws, strengthen confidence, face difficulties, work hard, and make new and greater contributions to realization of the Two Centenary Goals, and to achieving the Chinese Dream of great rejuvenation of the Chinese nation!